Civil War Echoes: Voices from Virginia, 1860–1891

CIVIL WAR ECHOES

VOICES FROM VIRGINIA, 1860–1891

James I. Robertson, Jr.

Virginia Sesquicentennial of the American Civil War Commission
Richmond, Virginia

©2016 by the
Virginia Sesquicentennial of
the American Civil War Commission

All rights reserved. First edition, published 2016.
Printed in the United States of America on acid-free paper.

ISBN 978-0-9834012-6-1

Virginia Sesquicentennial of the American Civil War Commission
Richmond, Virginia

www.VirginiaCivilWar.org

Contents

Preface	7
"How Hard the Life of a Soldier"	13
1861: "Drive Back the Dastard Invaders"	23
1862: "Consciousness of Right and Duty"	39
1863: "Our Loss Was Far Greater"	57
1864: "This Cruel War"	71
1865: "We Had a Hard Fite"	101
Epilogue: "The Fallen Leaves of the Forest"	117
Notes	121
Illustration credits	135
Index	137

PREFACE

Modern America emerged from four terrible years of civil war. To forget all of the ramifications of that struggle will imperil the future of American democracy. What happened yesterday directly affects what may occur tomorrow. That is why history is the best teacher the human race can ever have.

The years 2011–2015 marked the 150th anniversary of the nation's bloodiest war. Without question, the most successful commemoration came from the Virginia Sesquicentennial of the American Civil War Commission. The General Assembly created the Commission in 2006, and for the next decade it sponsored a wide variety of historic programs. One of the most enduring was the Civil War 150 Legacy Project: Digitization and Access.

Aware that many original Civil War materials such as letters, diaries, reminiscences, and photographs were in private hands, the Civil War Commission partnered with the Library of Virginia in an undertaking to locate and to preserve electronic copies of as many such documents as possible. The Legacy Project began in June 2010, with teams headed by two archivists crisscrossing the state and scanning memorabilia that Virginia citizens were willing to share with the public and with posterity.

The first copying began simultaneously in September 2010, in Charlotte County and Virginia Beach. Over the next two years, 141 scanning events occurred in almost every locality of the Commonwealth. Oftentimes people stood in line to have family documents copied. Holdings ranged from a single letter or photograph to huge collections of family papers. Library of Virginia personnel then digitized and catalogued the material into a single, usable collection.

Initial hopes were to amass perhaps 1,000 pages. What resulted was a primary historical reservoir of almost 33,000 digital images from 690 donors. The immense size of the collection is astounding, if not unprecedented. Yet its greatest value is in the richness of its contents.

Virginia was the major battlefield of the Civil War. Three of every five engagements took place on Old Dominion soil. No one can adequately describe the full destruction on such battlegrounds, but Lt. Richard Gaines, an assistant quartermaster, gave one of the detailed views when he visited the Second Manassas battlefield two days after the fighting.

"The ground is torn up by shot & shell, the trees are cut and torn & skewered, the grass & crops are scorched & burnt and trampled, and dead horses & men scattered in every direction. Sometimes here & there they can be counted by scores & hundreds. Our own men have all been buried, but the enemies killed in Thursday's, Friday's & Saturday's fights still lie stiff & cold & putrid black with mortification & some stripped entirely naked. Horrible, gastly & disgusting sights. Here and there over the field, by the side of branches and in the woods I counted seven parcels of yankee wounded which had been gathered up and had their wounds dressed by their surgeons, but not yet removed from the field. There they are without any thing to eat and no adequate means of any sort for their comfort."[1]

Often the battlefront and the home front were indistinguishable from one another. Destruction and domesticity were so entwined that the majority of Virginia families found it impossible to escape the wide-sweeping scythes of total war. Sometimes the contributions were overwhelming. In Fauquier County, three brothers in the Newlon family joined the 8th Virginia. All three died in a 13-month period.

The Old Dominion itself suffered more human-inflicted devastation than has befallen any other area in the Western Hemisphere.

Claudius W. Murdaugh, a Portsmouth native who took leave from the state legislature to serve in the Confederate army, observed in later years: "It was the boast of the ancient Greek, as his eye wandered over his beautiful and beloved land, that every hill bore the tomb of a hero or the temple of a God. We, of Virginia, if not the temple of a God, are the tomb of a hero."[2]

The war's inhuman machinery always drowned out human cries. Kindled emotions reveal far more about the Civil War than lines on a map or statistical charts. The forgotten human element is fundamental to a true understanding of the struggle for nationhood. Reading the story from the participants themselves gives the most soul-stirring and revealing picture we can ever have of those tumultuous times.

In May 2015, during the Sesquicentennial Commission's concluding program at the State Capitol, Speaker of the House of Delegates and Commission Chair William J. Howell announced that the huge manuscript collection from Virginia citizens would henceforth be known as the James I. Robertson, Jr., Legacy Project. The honoree urged that some of the material be published in book form for greater appeal and broader research purposes. Given the undying interest in human affairs, it is fitting that this volume is the Civil War Sesquicentennial Commission's final publication.

A major regret is the limitation on the amount of

material drawn from the Legacy Project for this book. Of some 1,700 collections, material was gleaned from less than 10 percent. To hold the published work to a single volume, only a third of the research notes were actually incorporated into the text. This reveals the enormity of the Legacy Project. Much quotable material awaits future researchers at the project's website, www.virginiamemory.com/collections/cw150.

To those who shared letters, journals, and reminiscences not mentioned here, please know that you still have the gratitude of all historically minded Americans for your generosity.

The narrators in this book were Confederate soldiers, Union soldiers on duty in the state, and Virginia citizens behind the lines. An opening chapter seeks to characterize the people of that time. Then, using the war years as a grid, a large choir recounts war experiences from start to end. Largely overlooked, these semi-educated "common folk" relate their stories of lost dreams, present anxieties, and future hopes that are rarely considered when looking back at the grand sweep of Civil War history.

Contrary to the norm, more letters and diaries exist for the last two years of the struggle than for the first 24 months. Excerpts are presented as they were written, with minor tweaks here and there for the sake of readability. Phonetic spelling (writing words the way they were spoken) has not been altered, to emphasize the lowly station in life whence so many came. Periods after sentences were inserted for the sake of clarity, and occasionally page-long narratives have been broken into paragraphs to facilitate continuity. In a few instances, the author inserted quotations from other sources to provide emphasis to thoughts and statements.

In 1882 poet and volunteer army nurse Walt Whitman lamented that the Civil War "was not a quadrille in the ballroom. Its interior history will not only never be written—its practicality, minutiae of deeds and passions will never even be suggested."³ Hopefully, this Civil War sesquicentennial collection will lessen the memory of the great bard's concern.

* * *

The members and staff of the Virginia Sesquicentennial of the American Civil War Commission deserve all the credit for the existence of the Legacy Project collection. Former delegate Al Eisenberg first raised the idea of a search for documents in private hands. Speaker of the House of Delegates William J. Howell, the Commission chair, strongly endorsed the concept and heartily oversaw the program through to the publication of this sample-volume. The Commission's executive director, Cheryl Jackson, took charge of the Legacy Project from conception to completion. Her dedication, as well as the driving force she brought to this book (and everything else pertaining to the Commonwealth's 150th anniversary remembrance), deserves highest praise.

Librarian of Virginia/State Archivist Sandra G. Treadway was enthusiastically cooperative at every stage. Her assistants at the Library of Virginia, notably Renee Savits and Laura Drake Davis, were in charge of collecting and cataloguing the flood of material. They performed hard work with diligence and efficiency.

Elizabeth Lee Robertson read the manuscript of this book with her usual thoroughness. An affectionate husband deeply appreciates her cheerful encouragement.

In the end, it was fellow Virginians (both native and adopted) who stepped forth to share nuggets of history for today and generations yet to come. Family pride, state loyalty, and love of country are powerful as well as beautiful assets for all Americans to cherish.

James I. Robertson, Jr.
"Eagle Rest"
Westmoreland County

"How Hard the Life of a Soldier"

History is the story of human beings. It should be the primary, most exciting avenue in the quest for knowledge because it chronicles the behavior of the most unpredictable of God's creatures. Yet too often history is presented as a collection of names, dates, statistics, and inanimate facts. The underlying element of history—emotion—is largely ignored. As a result, both the past and the present suffer.

Moreover, there exists in some quarters a misleading tendency to look at yesteryear through the lenses of today. Viewing nineteenth-century environment with twenty-first-century scrutiny uses the complex to measure the simple. The two ages were so radically different that pre–Civil War America cannot be fully understood until we realize the limited visions as well as the deep feelings of the time.

Of 27.5 million white Americans in 1860, half were under the age of 21. The nation was only 70 years old. It had not existed long enough to have wisdom. As it groped slowly down the road toward a national unity, the scope of the federal government and the presence of slavery in a democratic setting were the major issues.

Both soon created a heated atmosphere. States naturally possessed more maturity than the national government they created. Their instinctive fight to preserve state sovereignty was surprisingly successful. In 1860 the government at Washington directly touched a citizen only one way: it delivered the mail. Taxes and legal disputes were settled for the most part on state and local levels. The national budget relied on export and import duties.

Real nationalism lay beyond the horizon. None of the great avenues of transportation and communication were there as binding agents. Possibly 80 percent of Americans had never ventured beyond their home county. No national symbols existed to rally people to a common cause. The American flag flew only over public buildings and frontier outposts. There was no national anthem, no national motto, no national bird. (Benjamin Franklin's suggestion that the official bird be the buzzard gained much support because the average person had never seen an eagle.) America had faced no serious threat in its first seven decades. The powerful emotion of patriotism remained unborn. Hence, civil war in 1861 exploded on a people totally unprepared for it.

Virginia prewar society was comparable to that of the other, agriculturally dominated states. At the top of the economic ladder were the large landowners. In the Old Dominion, tobacco was the principal crop. Next in social status were the "poor folk" who fell into two classes: small farmers, herdsmen, and artisans who lived in a contented existence, and the poor whites whose talents were limited to menial labor, tenant farming, and simple work.

The plain-living but hardworking yeomen often resented the dominant elite class. However, as one historian concluded, "paternalism brought upper class and yeomen closer." The elite gave assistance; yeomen generally and "gratefully accepted such favors and in return upheld the social order without demanding social equality."[1]

An additional adhesive binding the social classes (of the North as well as the South) was the worldwide belief that black people were biologically inferior to whites. (Frederick

Douglass abolished that error.) Bondage was therefore a natural lot.

Betty Gray's diary reveals the shifting sentiments of owners toward their slaves. In May 1862, with the war entering its second year, Miss Gray wrote from her Fauquier County home: "The negro race is composed of curious and tretcherous people. Experience since the war [began] has tested the fact. Through their ignorance they are rejoicing at the present state of affairs & firmly believe the Yankee lyers who tell them they will be freer than their owners. But this Yankee freedom so sweet to some now will cause them, more trouble than they ever could imagine."

In the autumn of the following year, Gray noted that a friend from a neighboring home was staying with her. "After supper we sat in the kitchen with Black Mammie to hear her talk of old times. We have been begging her to remain with us all winter as she will have more comfortable quarters than with old husband Pete."[2]

For the true picture of the Civil War's impact, one must go not to the writings of generals and political leaders but to the soldiers in the ranks and their loved ones left at home. Most narratives of the war, a social historian stated, "keep the reader in perpetual motion, moving from battlefield to battlefield. . . . But that is not how the majority of the people engulfed by the war—southern civilians—experienced it. Most people, even the soldiers to a large extent, were spectators of the war, much like us."[3]

Two decades after the war, Capt. Claudius Murdaugh of the 61st Virginia voiced the same sentiments. "Narratives of personal adventure have a peculiar charm, and the unadorned tale of a soldier's hazards will often rivet the attention of those who would persevere through the more complicated and more important history of a great war."[4]

Most Johnny Rebs and Billy Yanks were away from home for the first time in their lives. Homesickness invariably overcame the first excitements. "I am nearly dead with the blues," the 1st Virginia Cavalry's Rudolphus Cecil confessed after a few months' service.[5]

Soldiers gravitated naturally from loneliness to letter writing. It was the only form of communication available. Given the strong emotions of the time, it should not be surprising that the Civil War gave rise to the greatest outpouring of letter writing in American history. From camp near Orange, Middlesex artilleryman John Clarke told his sweetheart: "A soldier in the field is greatly comforted to know that there is one that thinks of him while he is so subject to trials and difficulties that are so numerous in the life of a soldier. You would doubtless not believe me were it possible for me to tell you how hard the life of a soldier was."[6]

In October 1862, Thomas W. Fisher of the 51st Virginia somewhat humorously informed his wife in Wytheville that the soldiers' only complaint is "they don't get letters enough. [John G.] Cameron offered me [a] quarter for my letter to day after I had read it. He said he had not got one for so long that he would have to buy of some body or else he would not get none atall. James Harrell says if he don't get one he intended to write a long one and take it home and let his wife read it and then bring the answer back."[7]

At the same time, and more poignantly, Henry County soldier John Stone confessed to his wife, "I shed tears ever time I get a letter from you." Two months later, Stone added, "Martha Ann, I Dream about you and the children most ever night."[8]

Letters from home possessed equally deep sentiments. Jane Watkins Gaines wrote her husband from Charlotte County in the spring of 1862: "I pray that God will bring you safely back to me and our dear little children, when you have accomplished the work which I believe he has given you to do. I long to see you with feelings inexpressible, but I try to be resigned and patient."[9]

At some point in the war, Jane Adams Oden composed a poem to her husband, John, a surgeon in the 2nd

Unidentified woman, ca. 1860–1870. From her gown and jewelry, it is obvious that this woman was from an affluent family. A photograph of a wife or sweetheart was a Civil War soldier's most prized possession.

Virginia Cavalry:

> Thou art ever present with me,
> Although wand'ring far away,
> For I dream of naught besides thee
> Throughout all the weary day.
> In my heart thy image resteth,
> Guarded close by tender love,
> Whose white banner ever waveth—
> The sweet memory above.
> . . . .
> And art thou, *My darling*, keeping
> In thy heart a thought of me—
> Art thou ever fondly dreaming
> Of the love I gave to thee?[10]

Mail delivery was sporadic at best, and long intervals between letters brought fears of the unknown. The sight of a communication from home provided high excitement, unless the letter bore the worst possible news. Such a communiqué James Warwick of the 11th Virginia Cavalry wrote on May 13, 1864, to "Miss Maggie":

"It now becomes my most painful duty . . . to communicate to you the sad intelligence of the death of your Brother James, who was killed one week ago today while nobly discharging the duties of a soldier, in an engagement with the enemy near Verdiersville, Orange County. The fight commenced about 8 o'clock in the morning and he was shot about eleven, by a large minnie ball penetrating the skull, entering in the forehead just above the right eye. He was not conscious after being shot of anything atall, but lived about two hours and a half. He was very neatly interred in about two miles of where he was shot, near a Mrs Faulkner's on what is called the Cathoppin road. . . . I have charge of his horse, coat, Port-monail &c. You will find enclosed in this letter a ring that I found in his Port-monail & also a lock of hair."[11]

More lasting and treasured than a letter was a photograph of a loved one. Photography was only 30 years old when civil war began. Yet rapid technical advances, especially the process that yielded inexpensive paper prints, made it possible for ordinary citizens to have a likeness made.

Sprinkled throughout this volume are examples of individual photographs, or "cartes de visite," as they were called. After receiving such a photograph from his wife, Maj. Henry DeShields responded: "You cant imagine what a real comfort your picture is to me. Shall I tell you that I kiss it many times a day—it looks so natural sometimes that it seems to me to *know* that I am kissing it. I wish it could speak to me, but it is a treasure as it is."[12]

The greatest enemy faced by Civil War soldiers was sickness. Medical knowledge was still lodged in the Middle Ages. Breakthrough discoveries in bacteriology and sanitation did not occur in America until a decade after the war. Hence, if people were not sick, they were constantly anxious of becoming so. And because of lack of immunity in the population, every outbreak of disease moved unencumbered to epidemic proportions.

Diarrhea was the most common illness—and the biggest killer in the struggle. A Bedford County recruit had been in service but four months when he wrote fearfully that he "had rather face the Yankees than the sickness and there is allways more men dies from sickness than in battle."[13]

From camp near Warrenton in the spring of 1862, H. C. Lawton of the 2nd Rhode Island informed his cousin: "I have had a very hard time with the diaareha and have not got rid of it yet. I have lost flesh awfully lately, you would hardly know me. . . . I cant write much I am so weak."[14]

Charles W. Thomas spent most of his service with the 56th Virginia in battling intestinal disorders. "My bowels are very much out of fix," he declared in May 1863. "I am discharging coal for several days but I keep up with the ballance." The following summer, Thomas was down again. "I thaut some time ago that I was going to be tolerable well [but] I weakened down so fast that I went to the hospital."[15] Thomas died of pneumonia in April 1865 while a prisoner of war at Point Lookout, Maryland.

In every military hospital, the most frequently listed cause of death was "Diarrhea Chron[ic]."[16]

Modern-day physicians know the word to describe a symptom more than a disease. Inadequate nutrition and uncontrollable infection made bowel disorder a scourge in every encampment. Men in the ranks came to say that one "had to have good guts to be a soldier."[17]

Typhoid fever was the second most deadly disease. The 18th Virginia participated in three years of combat duty, yet it suffered more deaths from "back bone fever" than from battle. The malady struck early and killed often. Sergeant Milton Runkle of the 34th Virginia wrote his cousin in the first autumn of the war: "The Fever is raging in camp pickens now. At this time we have three in our Comp down with it. . . . Our [100-man] company is down to fifty men and some of them is complaining."[18]

Vaccination for smallpox was in its infancy, so fears of the disease were constant. Near the end of 1862, while on duty near Bull Run, soldier Alexander Seiders told his wife: "Smallpox is verry Bade here. We have Bearray'd 2 yesterday. A gane 8 or 9 dide here of the small pox. I am well at present and if should happen to get sick I wount take no medson of dockter as long as I can croall but I hope I wount get sick."[19]

Inoculation for the disease was generally crude. In January 1862, Private Thomas of the 56th Virginia told his wife in Mecklenburg County: "I send you some scabs of my Arm where I ware vascinated for the small pox. You must soften them with water & put some in the hole familys arms."[20]

Rubeola, the most infectious of today's "childhood" diseases, was the first malady to sweep through the ranks.

Red measles, as it is commonly called, can be fatal because of the ease with which it can enter the lungs and produce pneumonia. Survival in the Civil War era depended on luck rather than treatment. In October 1861 a Floyd County farmer-turned-soldier announced to a family member: "I hav bin tolable well except bad cols. The measles is in me yet, I no be cause I can smell them when I hav a cole."[21]

No genuine remedy existed for any disease. Yet concoctions were many. One "prescription" for whooping cough was: "Dissolve a scruple of salt of tartar in a ¼ pint of water. Add 10 grains of cochineal, finely powdered, sweeten with fine white sugar. For an infant ¼ tablespoonful four times a day. A child 2 or 3 years old ½ a spoonful."[22]

The most recurring theme in Virginia Confederate writings is expression of faith. While a wide divergence might exist between a preacher's exhortation and the congregation's response, "religious sanction was demanded by the righteous, approved by the lukewarm, and tolerated by the wicked. All felt better to have the blessing of the church."[23] Belief in God and the Hereafter proved to be the greatest motivation in the maintenance of soldier and civilian morale.

Writing from Drewry's Bluff in September 1862, John H. Stone told his Henry County family: "I hope I will return back home agan. I must look to God for all my help. God is the only true friend we have." Aquilla Peyton of the 30th Virginia echoed those sentiments the following spring: "I dread the horrid work [of a soldier]. Faith in God, however, is all I need."[24]

Religious exercises, prayer meetings, revival services, and baptisms became common scenes in Southern armies, especially in the latter half of the war. Soldiers found strength in the biblical text: "Greater love hath no man than this, that a man lay down his life for his friends."[25] They did not hesitate to ask for moral support from their families. "I desire an interest in all your prayers," the 51st Virginia's Thomas Fisher wrote, "that I may be one of the happy ones that shall return home after this storm of war has blown over."[26] Fisher was blessed and survived the war.

Samuel Garrett of the 3rd Virginia Cavalry was convinced that the genuineness of Confederate faith would bring ultimate victory. He stated in an undated 1862 letter: "At the north the pulpit has been perverted and corrupted for partisan purposes & instead of the gospel fanaticism alone is preached. Here the people at least seem to place their trust in God and a feeling of deep faith pervades every community."[27]

Naturally, Virginia troops speculated about the future. Just before the opening of the 1864 Wilderness campaign, James T. Blair of the 5th Virginia envisioned a rough road to ultimate triumph. "The hottest battle of the war will be fought shortly and it will take sad news to many a poor soldier's home. I hope that God will spare me and let me live to see home once more and that we can tell the world that we have established our Confederate Government and gained an honorable peace, but still before this can be done, we will have to go through many hardships and suffer many privations."[28]

Blair was killed September 22, 1864, at the battle of Fisher's Hill.

In 1860 the Old Dominion had a history three times longer than that of the United States. Its citizens were more Virginian than American when disunion brought war. A sad irony appeared when residents of the Mother State faced a conflict that could destroy forever the nation their forefathers had done so much to create.

1861
"Drive Back the Dastard Invaders"

A civil war takes a long time to unfold. That the participants live in the same land, speak the same language, have the same traditions, faith, customs, and hopes, makes it difficult to get citizens in a mood to start killing each other. Years of passionate debate eventually produce a spark, then another. Heat—both physical and mental—leads to explosions, and the bloodiest kind of war results.

Following John Brown's unprovoked attack on Harpers Ferry, Virginia, in October 1859, a Prince George County matron stated that "there was great unrest thro the entire South."[1] Militia companies formed in every Virginia community for defense against other possible terrorist raids. The 1860 presidential election of Abraham Lincoln and a Republican Party opposed to the expansion of slavery in the United States appeared to be the final political cleavage. South Carolina led an exodus of seven states from the Union. They in turn established the Confederate States of America.

The Deep South had much bluster but little capability for war. Central to any Southern success were the three states between Union and Confederacy. Virginia, together with Tennessee and North Carolina, contained half the population of what became the Confederacy. Their products of food and livestock, plus their industrial output, dwarfed that of the original bloc of seven states. In truth, the future of the Southern attempt at independence lay in what action Virginia took.

Like its southern sisters, the Old Dominion created a secession convention to determine its future course. Even before it officially convened, State Sen. Alexander H. H. Stuart of Staunton asserted that "nine-tenths" of the state legislature had "gone crazy" in the rush to abandon the Union. Stuart added: "Madness rules the hour. You can hardly imagine the insanity."[2]

Fortunately, moderates formed a majority in the convention. Little enthusiasm for secession existed. In March 1861, a Tennessee physician made a political diagnosis that "the fever [in Virginia] is gradually subsiding—and soon our sick patient will be convalescent." Another observer stated: "Without some decidedly and unequivalently hostile demonstration by the [Lincoln] administration, *immediate secession* in Virginia is as dead as a door nail."[3]

The situation changed explosively. Late on Saturday afternoon, April 13, telegraphic dispatches reached Richmond of Confederate batteries bombarding Union-held Fort Sumter in the harbor of Charleston, South Carolina. Enthusiastic mobs swept through Richmond streets. A Confederate flag soon waved over the State Capitol. One cheering crowd dragged cannon from the arsenal and fired a 100-gun salute to the new banner. Unionists scrambled to take cover.

Abraham Lincoln reacted differently to the Fort Sumter surrender. He issued a call for 75,000 state militia to report for 90-day service. Their aim was to put down an insurrection "too powerful to be suppressed by the ordinary course of judicial proceedings."[4] Obviously, to Southerners, Lincoln's intent was to send those Union forces through Virginia to finish the work that John Brown had begun.

"At once the whole state turned in favor of secession," wrote Elizabeth Callender in Prince George County.[5] Federals would ignore state sovereignty and cross Virginia's border without permission. This was blatant coercion. The secession convention thereupon voted 88–55 to disengage itself from such "usurpers of the Constitution."

Fauquier County's Betty Gray voiced popular support when she noted in her journal: "Three cheers for brave Virginia / The Old Dominion State / With the Young Confederacy / At length has linked her fate."[6]

Other responses had a more somber tone. "War, grim-visaged war, has at length reared its horrid front amongst us," one editor proclaimed. "That greatest of all human calamities, civil war, is . . . absolutely upon us."[7] William L. Goggin, a Bedford County representative to the secession convention, returned home and gave a speech at the courthouse. "When he told the people with tears in his eyes how he eyed the result, Goggin broke down and wept like a child over the condition of the country. There were not many dry eyes in the crowd that evening."[8]

Margaret Moss Agee wrote of troops mustering in Cumberland County and concluded: "No body is doing any business now. All is trouble & confusion. . . . Many be the tears that I shed on account of our approaching desolation."[9]

And so, after years of antagonisms, the long wait was over. Strong debates over the dividing line between state and federal control, plus the continuance of slavery, had led to warfare. Americans had always prided themselves on a reputation for pragmatism and a reliance on compromise. The two principles no longer existed. Emotion had replaced reason. Now, in what was a relief to many people, the contest would shift from politicians to soldiers. American democracy had failed.

In the beginning, the North overestimated unionism in the South. Federals assumed that secession was not a popular political movement but an aristocratic action non-slaveholding Southerners would not support. What sent Southerners to battle in 1861 was the deep conviction to defend home and loved ones. Virginia volunteers, a Mecklenburg County newspaper announced, "go to the post of danger with stout hearts and determined spirits, resolved to drive back the dastard invaders from the consecrated soil of Virginia, or to die in the attempt."[10]

Henry DeShields was practicing law in Heathsville when war began. To his wife then in Dinwiddie County he wrote: "I think by to-morrow night I shall have succeeded (with others) in getting up a fine volunteer company for service in the Northern Neck. . . . I found everybody here had been terribly frightened . . . & few disposed to *volunteer*. . . . I made a speech of 3/4 hour a few hours after I reached here & it made me very hoarse for some days to come."[11]

Skepticism existed too in those first emotions of war. Austin Edwards, who lived in the Whitmell district of Pittsylvania County, heard from his brother: "I have thought all of My life untill Now That I lived in a civilised Land. But Look at things that happen right a round us and Especially at those that are in power in Washington city, and I very Naturally conclude that I am in a Land of Barbarians. . . . It is raily a very distressing time, the people over this way don't seem to think about much Else but war."[12]

Andrew Nye lived in southwest Virginia's isolated Giles County. His observations were limited to rumors and the nearby railroad. "Every train is loaded with troops, fine looking men," Nye wrote his son in early May. "They are all a merry set and anxious to get hold of Lincoln or [Winfield] Scott. . . . The volenteers have a song that they sing on the Carrs: Lincoln is mad and I am glad, Whoza for old Virginia."

Nye then revealed how far-fetched rumor could be. "All of the Public buildings in Washington has been mined (powder placed under them ready to blow them up) provided they have to retreat from Washington. Scott is said to be sick and Lincoln has his cloak and cap ready to leave. There doctrine is to exterminate all males and force the white women to marry negroes and yankeys and give them the soil of the South."[13]

Opposition to the war was ever present in areas of the state. David Myrick enlisted early in a company that became part of the 6th Virginia. However, his sister Helen wrote that not everyone in Southampton County shared his fervor. "Some of the people . . . say that they will not go to war. Before they do they will cut their throats—from ear to ear—but it is some of the illiterate ones. I do hope our Southern men will be brave. I feel so much, think so much, that sometimes I hardly feel myself."[14]

Dazzled in part by orators who promised that Virginians "just had to kick the Yankees out of the way with buckshot and cornstalks," thousands answered the call to arms "with a boyhood ardor and patriot's conviction."[15] Samuel Garrett of Cumberland County was among that group. After his company left home to become part of the 3rd Virginia Cavalry, Garrett reassured his wife: "You seemed to speak very despondingly of our cause in your last letter. Altho' it is true we are out numbered by the north yet even they are beginning to see the difference between a horde of rowdies & a more compact and well disciplined army who have their homes, kindred, wives & children to defend, and as sure as our father in whom we put our trust lives and rules, we will beat them and that badly."[16]

The route to becoming a real soldier lay in drill, drill, and more drill. For almost three years the 39th Massachusetts served in Virginia. Freeman Colby of that unit would later state: "Most of our time was devoted to drilling, which was most necessary, for none of us had any military experience. . . . Some took the training with sober industry and diligently tried to learn all they could, while others never realized until long afterwards that [this] was anything but a picnic frolic."[17]

Camp Lee, on the fairgrounds west of downtown Richmond, became the largest training camp for Virginia volunteers. Cadets from the Virginia Military Institute

A boastful air characterizes the cavalryman that Joseph Lee Minghini was. Born in March 1837 near Shepherdstown, Minghini enlisted in the 12th Virginia Cavalry. He served as a courier for Gen. "Jeb" Stuart until his December 1863 discharge from the service. Minghini resided in Martinsburg until his death in January 1919.

served as drillmasters. The 1st Virginia's Howard Walthall remembered: "Streets were formed of tents all over the immense grounds and it was a great show place for the citizens who came out to visit and witness our maneuvers. The girls were largely in evidence at the afternoon dress parades and the Richmond boys were the envy of those from country towns because every one had a girl or two to smile on him and escort him to their homes whilst the other poor fellows had to stay in camp and go to bed at taps. That month seemed a long one to many because we thought the enemy would get away before we had a chance to go for them and we were getting very tired of that everlasting drilling under those squirty little cadets who lorded it over us like they were seasoned soldiers."[18]

Harpers Ferry was the northernmost point of the Confederacy. The confluence there of the Potomac and Shenandoah Rivers gave it high strategic value. It too became a concentration point for recruits, even though it lacked the luster and appeal of Camp Lee. Late in May, an Alabama volunteer told his family: "We . . . have seen a great many natural curiosities . . . there is some sickness in camp: Colds, Measles & Mumps. There is over 12000 soldiers at this place & still they come. We begin to feel we will suffer for want of provisions. Our Rations are not equal to our appetites.

"Old Abe has given us 24 hours to leave this place. I think he ought to have given us more time to pack our goods. As he has not, we will wait and give him a warm reception."[19]

To miss the strong family ties present in the Civil War is to miss appreciably the depth of that period's emotions. This was especially so in those first weeks of the struggle, when menfolk left to fight with uncertainty about the feelings and safety of family left at home.

Many wives gave prompt reassurances. Mary Thomas of Mecklenburg County sent her husband a loving report of herself and their three children. "Bettie very often asks Ma tars Pa & when answered [he has] gone to fight the yankeys, she will say Me want to see Pa so bad me don't know what do. . . . The other two does not say much about you but when your name is called we know by the tears in their little eyes that they feel if they do not speak. Don't give yourself one moments uneasiness about us. We are doing well and are as well satisfied as any one could expect to be under the present circumstances."[20]

Both sides were overanxious to fight the battle that would end the war. On Sunday, July 21, two armed mobs calling themselves armies collided in an all-day engagement along Bull Run near Manassas. Hundreds of Washington civilians rode out in buggies and with picnic baskets to see the Civil War become history. Instead, a brilliant stand at a critical moment by troops under Gen. Thomas "Stonewall" Jackson, followed by a timely counterattack by fresh regiments, brought stunning victory to the Confederate cause.

The 1st Virginia Cavalry's John Ervine wrote his wife: "It is true a man in this place [Manassas] told me he seen a part of the congress & secretary [Simon] Cameron also go up & many Ladies or rather women. They fully calculate[d] on whiping us & having a barbecue at [Manassas] Junction next day."[21]

Richmond soldier Howard Walthall wrote proudly that "a decisive battle occurred with great disaster to the enemy. They realized the fighting metal of men defending their homes and their determination to drive them back at all hazards and seeing the havoc produced in their ranks, became panic stricken and fled for their lives, leaving guns, ammunition, small arms and everything that would impede their progress. It was an amazing as well as ludicrous sight when we got near enough to understand the situation. The roads and fields were blocked with material that hardly seemed necessary for fighting, besides vast stores of army rations. There were house hold goods, overturned private carriages and other things which indicated the invaders were out for a good time and expected a regular walk over and had brought along all sorts of comforts & conveniences for enjoying their little outing. We were so elated at their downfall and our victory over superior numbers."[22]

After the battle of First Manassas (or First Bull Run, as it was called in the North), Southerners waited for peace overtures. Lincoln thought otherwise. The American union is perpetual, he asserted. It cannot be broken by the whims of a minority of citizens.

Thus, while the Confederate states languished in the autumn of 1861, the Union began large-scale preparations for a long war. New York City recruit Frederick Watkins told his brother that he had "enlisted in to the service of my Country, not to bolster up the Black Republican Party, but to support our Glorious Constitution, to preserve this Union unbroken."[23]

Part of the North's strategy was to secure strategic footholds in Virginia. When Federal troops marched into the Eastern Shore, Gen. John Dix gave peaceful assurances to residents that his men would "go among you as friends, and with the earnest hope that they may not by your own acts be forced to become your enemies. . . . They will invade no rights of person or property, or interfere with any of your lawful rights or your social and local institutions."[24]

Federals did not always display such courtesies. Less than a week after the Manassas battle, Sgt. John Ervine was with the 1st Virginia Cavalry on a patrol in northern Virginia. "The yankeys have destroyed all the property in this part of the country," he noted. "Along the roads some houses have not a single pair of goblets in them. Not one of them have any clothing or furniture. . . . [They] have carried off all the negros that they coul. I herd of one or two that said they would be shot before they would go. Consequently they were left."[25]

A month later, Abraham Vanfleet of the 1st New Jersey was part of a detail that seized some earthworks in the Alexandria-Springfield region. Vanfleet relished what followed. "Our officers went into the deserted houses to get things, and the first thing I saw was our doctor was coming on his horse with two pigs, one on each side of his horse and they were squealing very hard . . . by and by our chaplain came with a lot of chickens, then the doctor went back and got a calf. That day we got about 12 tons of hay, 12 cows and a lot of calves, chickens, geese, cabbage, and a lot of furniture."[26]

During the six-month lull following the Manassas shootout, some soldiers got to experience new sites and events. Fred Watkins of the 4th New York Light Artillery was stationed on Arlington Heights. One autumn afternoon he visited the new Capitol building under construction. "Outside it appears in a very unfinished state," he wrote his mother in New York City, "the parts more immediately striking the eye, being the great central dome and the grand marble entrances to the new wings containing the new Senate Chamber and House of Representatives, which are not half done, the ground around being strewn with huge marble blocks and pillars, and iron castings for the dome.

"The old house now forms a sort of ante-chamber to the new one, and appears most diminutive in comparison. The new house as well as the Senate Chamber is lighted at night, as well as the daytime from above: the gaslights being introduced between the stained glass ceiling and the glass roof over it making a most soft and agreable light. The halls and corridors are most elegantly paved with mosaic and with the handsome decorations and spacious dimenshions of their interior make a fitting place for the assemblage of the Congress of a free and mighty nation of Sovereigns."[27]

A Confederate private was disappointed at the appearance of his capital city. "Richmond is a poor place this time to think about seeing any fun . . . one thing I am cirtain of, and that is that there is mean whisky and beef enough and these are the only articles that are plentiful."[28]

Another Confederate was fascinated at the growing

number of captured soldiers in Richmond. "I saw over 1700 Yankee Prisoners . . . but of course could not speak to them. There were 74 Prisoners brought in yesterday. Some are wounded, some are waiting on them, some stand in groups talking, some sit off to themselves & look very serious, some are cheerful & some are gritting their teeth & shaking their fists at the boys in the streets."[29]

Washington, D. C., appeared even less appealing. A member of the 1st Massachusetts Heavy Artillery wrote after his arrival at the Northern capital: "The three splended buildings of the capitol are neither of them finished. In front and in the rear of the capitol is a splended park but with the exception of these the place near the capital is covered with old shanties and barnes, heaps of stone, brick and old lumber all through the city. Hogs and geese are let to run loose in the streets. Ther is but one decent street . . . and that is Penselvania av."[30]

When Joseph Embrey of the 13th Virginia visited Winchester for the first time, he was impressed. "I have bin to church to day and herd a verry fine sermon," Embrey wrote his sister. "I walked with the prettyest girl you ever saw. If I could *stay with her all ways I would not care if peaches never got ripe*. There is the prettyest girls in this place I ever saw in my life. You ote to see them."[31]

Embrey died of disease six weeks later.

Lack of female companionship produced equally strong comments. Greene County's Milton Runkle and his 34th Virginia were stationed at Camp Pickens near the Potomac River. He told a kinsman: "I should like to see those fare faces that I cannot see here. I have not seen but four or five women since I have been here. Very lonesome here in the line of ladies. . . . You must tell the girls for me they must not all get married to the Malitia before I get back there. Some one of them must save themselvs for me."[32]

Rumors constantly circulated through every encampment. James Newlon wrote his parents in Loudoun

County: "I have just heard that the yankees have taken Leesburg but I dont be leave it. I hear so much that I dont beleave half that I hear."[33]

The occasional appearance in camp of newspapers did little to clarify the situation. Arthur C. Cummings, who became colonel of the 33rd Virginia, wrote a Winchester friend: "I need scarcely attempt to give you the news as you will see more in the papers than I could give you—one half of which is not true and one half of the remaining half exaggerated." Massachusetts soldier Lewis Holt echoed the same sentiments. "You get twice as much news as we do out here," he wrote home. "It is impossible for you to know how the papers lie. They get short of news and make up a lie out of whole cloth."[34]

Chilly weather of autumn brought waves of sickness to army encampments. Confederates abandoned the Bull Run line because the water became too contaminated even to smell. "This part of the country is very near ruined," a Southern private asserted. "There has been a great many of our men sick since we have been here, and there are several sick yet. I have been right bad off but am able to go on duty again."[35]

Civil War soldiers were in the main farm boys scattered all over the land. Few had acquired any immunity to what are called today "childhood" or "urban" diseases. In filthy encampments of thousands of unwashed soldiers jammed together, and with medical knowledge still at primitive level, any communicable disease became an epidemic.

"Mary, I am sorry to tell you we lost another of our men yestady, which had the measles," the 56th Virginia's Charles Thomas wrote his wife. "His name was Wesley House. He were at the hors pittle and nearly got well and got up night before last wich was Friday. Sent a negro out and bought a very large water mellon and ate it. He then was taken with a chill and had three by the next morning. The last

Born in 1843, John Floyd Walker enlisted August 8, 1861, in the "Botetourt Guards" of the 57th Virginia. He served the entire war and surrendered at Appomattox. Until his death in 1904, Walker was a successful farmer in Giles County.

one kiled him, so he kiled himself."[36]

In August, a concerned woman published a broadside that begged all residents of the Manassas area to contribute "supplies for the sick and wounded" at local soldier-hospitals. "We must all feel that the aching head and throbbing pain need those comforts which is the privilege of women to devise and supply. . . . Is there a woman in Virginia who is not willing to make some sacrifice to accomplish this object?"[37]

Behind the lines all across the state, health conditions oftentimes were just as severe. Mrs. Ellen Ervine of Rockbridge County informed her husband in the 1st Virginia Cavalry that typhoid fever was raging through the countryside. Their son Lewis was near death. "One of Tarlton Campbells sons was buried yesterday. . . . He had Typhoid Fever, got better of that, took Black Tongue and died in 36 hours after taking it. Dr Hamilton says he never witness'd a more dreadful death. . . . If that should break out amongst us with ev'ry thing else, we might as well give up."[38]

Being placed in primitive army hospital care could increase a soldier's misery. "It is very bad to be sick away from home," George Newlon of the 8th Virginia confessed. "I never want to be sick away from home again if I can help it. I am treated very well by the nurses but the fair is very bad . . . I dont get more than half enough."[39]

From a Richmond hospital on Christmas Day, North Carolina soldier Charles Lasley informed his father: "I want to get away from here pretty soon if I dont take the Mumps but I am afraid I shall for they are in my room. The Itch is also in the room, and if I get the mumps and Itch too I shall stay here untill February."[40]

Less than 100 miles from Richmond, the North was molding what would become the largest army ever seen in the Western Hemisphere. At its head was charismatic but cautious Gen. George McClellan. He proved to be a great morale-builder, and his troops adored him.[41]

Meanwhile, Confederate soldiers in Virginia fortified

key points and awaited developments. On December 9, Southern soldiers got their first (but hardly their last) look at extreme military justice. Two Louisiana privates were executed for assault and insubordination. The division to which the 8th Virginia belonged was ordered to form ranks and witness the punishment. James Newlon described the scene in a letter to his aunt in Chesterfield County.

"I saw two of the louisiana tigers shot last Monday week. I was close to one of them. He did not seem to mind it. He laught & talked with the guard as thay went to the field. He had a chain & ball on. Thay tide thre hand behind them & tied them to a stake. There was twenty four men detaled to shoot them. Twelve guns were loded with balls & twelve were loded with blank cartridges. One of them was kiled ded & the other one live five or ten minuts."[42]

Probes and skirmishes occasionally broke the tedium of camp life. In the western Virginia counties, real fighting marked late 1861. Control of a third of the Commonwealth was at issue. One such skirmish occurred December 13, when Federals assaulted the Confederate outpost at Camp Allegheny near Greenbrier. Joseph W. Campbell, an Augusta County native and member of the 52nd Virginia, wrote an account of the action for his cousin. The letter is a remarkable example of Civil War phonetic spelling.

"I wood of ritten yesterday but yesterday morning before sun up they yankees came on ous. Thay had ous vary neir serrounded. The was a bout 3000 yankees and a bout 1000 of our men. We had tow fights. The yankees devi[d]ed and went tow ways. Our Regimet was in the ditches. I was in frount of the battle the hole time. The yankees had the advantedg of our men. thay got in the tree tops behind logs and behind stumps so that we cood not see them. When wey wod look over the bank thay wod shoot at ous. I was vary neare give out when I got to the ditches. It was the first time I had ben out eny distance for soum time. I had no order to go but I went and took good ame at the yankees but I ca[n]t say that I kiled eny. The balls fell like hale. The Yankees kiled a good meny of our oficers. . . . We faugt a bout 6 hors and hafe."[43]

The war's first Christmas brought happy thoughts as well as feelings of frustration and loneliness. Aquilla Peyton, a pious recruit from Fredericksburg, noted disgustedly: "I have not mentioned Christmas. It passed rather quietly. There was some drunkenness, however, and a good many took 'French furloughs.'"[44]

Essex County's Muscoe Brooks was a member of the 55th Virginia. On Christmas Eve, he wrote his fiancée: "I wish for the time to come [home] this Christmas but I am sory times is bad so we cannot get maried this Christmas but I hope the time will soon come when we can get maried if it is your wishes. . . . My Dear I [had] rather see you than any one in this world. Oh how hapy I should be. Oh I love you beter than any one in this wourld. The last leter I rote to you it was so badly riten and I had no in velops nor nothin to seal it up with. It look so bad I am afraid that you was displease with me about it."[45] Eight months later, Brooks was mortally wounded at the battle of Second Manassas.

Throughout the winter encampments, faith in God sustained many of those impressionable young men. Charles Thomas of the 56th Virginia admitted to his wife: "You requested of me to prepare to meet my god, for which I am trying to do. I want you, if you ant, to do the same. I ant curst a oath in some time and stop drinkin in a measure & are praying to god for his assistance."[46]

1862
"Consciousness of Right and Duty"

Winter seasons always brought suffering. "We have Rain or Snow nearly every day," Alabama soldier John Adams wrote from Dumfries. "At this time the snow is nearly a foot Deep, the Sun is shining & the Snow melting, which makes it verry disagreeable especially to one who wears Shoes."[1]

Sickness accentuated weather miseries. Thomas Newlon wrote his parents from Centreville: "I am not very well at present and have not been well . . . since I come down. I have a very bad cough at this time and I have a bile on the side of my neck which trouble me very much." At the same time, in the Shenandoah Valley, the 52nd Virginia's Adam Kersh explained why he had not written home of late. "I have had the jaunders working on me for about eight days now which makes me feel very lowlifed and mean. They have come out on me now. I look about as yellow as a pompkin."[2]

Families at home also battled disease. Germs brought from an army camp could have disastrous effects. In March, Mary Allen of Amherst County tearfully informed her soldier-son of the sudden deaths of his two nephews. "I have the sad news to tell you that I had to part from my dear little Joshua and little Willie. The good Lord taken them bouth from me. Willie died on the 16 and Joshua on the 20 only 4 days between thair deaths. Joshua live only 4 days after taken sick and little Willie about the same. Poor little children bouth died entirly out of thair right minds. They died speachless. Oh my dear son I am allmost Heart broaken. . . . The Dr pronounces thair disease Camp fever [typhoid fever]. I have regrated a thousand times that William ever went to manassas as he brought the fever with him. A few days after William was taken sick. It took t[w]o men to hole him in his room. He was entirley derange for very ny a week."[3]

Homesickness was constant in every encampment, and it took various forms. Boredom was one mold. After the 13th Massachusetts spent almost a year of inactivity in northern Virginia, Pvt. David Hicks complained that "the romance of soldiering is about played out with the most of us, and there is left only the stern realities of irksome routine." Nathan Cox, whose 29th Virginia was isolated in the remote southwestern quadrant of the state, concluded, "We dont no much More about what is going on away from here than a man in Jail."[4]

Absence of females also lowered spirits. The 45th North Carolina's William Baughn lived just across the border from Henry County, Virginia. Ten months into the war, Baughn wrote with resignation: "I have been away from the gals so long that I do not care so much to be with them. I have forgotten how to talk to them. I havent spoken two doesen words to them since I left Suffolk."[5]

Milton Runkle, a sergeant in the 34th Virginia, was more upbeat. Answering a cousin's letter, Runkle declared: "You say every thing [in Greene County] is high but girls. I suppose they are very cheap. When I get hom I will put in A special requisitian for three or four. . . . I have been very lonesome here, not [a] girl to be seen."[6]

Adversities might momentarily dampen patriotic spirits, but they could not cripple the devotion to state so deeply rooted in the Virginians. During the fall and winter of 1861–1862, additional military units were formed; earthen fortifications were strengthened at dozens of strategic points; Richmond "wore a martial air, the streets were crowded with soldiers marching in companies and regiments, all intent on preparations for defence."[7]

What sustained the majority of Virginia citizens was the belief—more than a hope—that the Yankees would eventually be driven back for good across the Potomac. A Union private, writing from Middleburg, described the locals as "Secesh to the *bare bone*. They say the Southern people will never give up, until everything is entirely sacrificed."[8]

Richard Gaines left his 800-acre farm in Charlotte County to become a lieutenant in the Staunton Hill Artillery. He explained to his wife why he had to fight. "Nothing but a stern sense of duty could make me take the position which has fallen to my lot. I could not consent to play the part of a drone or laggard in this great contest and however great may be the sacrifices and trials which I may encounter, the consciousness of right and duty will enable me to meet them cheerfully."[9]

Combat resumed in March when Federal forces occupied Winchester in the lower end of the Shenandoah Valley. New England soldier David Hicks described the Union arrival. "Our Army marched into the town with bands playing and colors flying. It was interesting to note the anxious careworn faces of the people as they eagerly scanned our faces, evidently expecting to see the blood thirsty monsters we had been represented to be. I heard two or three ladies say, 'O! look at the colors! Arnt they pretty' with an earnestness that told how they had watched and waited for that sign from the East, that sign of peace and plenty of glory and power. Yes, there were many handkerchiefs waving and many eyes full of tears."[10]

A month later, Union troops forced Confederates to evacuate Fredericksburg. James Scates of the 40th Virginia recalled the bittersweet feelings in having to abandon the port city. "We being largely outnumbered we was ordered to retreat until we could reenforce. We then Set fire to the three bridges crossing the Rappahanock River and all the Steam boats and vessels about Fredericksburg and we began our retreat. Then followed a scene long to be remembered. The clouds of smoke and the roar of the rageing fire of the burning bridges and vessels could be seen and heard for miles on our march. Scarcely had we crossed over and set fire to the bridges before the yankeys came in sight on the other side. . . . [They] fired several cannon at us and killed a horse under one of our cavalry men."[11]

In Union-held Warrenton, a young diarist noted: "Lovely Sabbath has passed & no sounds of the church bell has greated mine ear. It seemes we are in a heathen land. Truly 'tis not much better. Only Yankee land."[12]

Frances Fisher lived in Wytheville, far from the battle arenas. Her overriding concern was her husband, Thomas. Eight days earlier, he had left her and their three small children to join the army. Mrs. Fisher suddenly learned that spring fighting had started, whereupon she sent a long, rambling, and revealing letter. "There was a dispatch come to town Wednesday that they was a fiting at richmond but we aint heard yet how they made it. . . . I did know how meny was kiled on our side but I forgot. I heard that if our side whiped at richmond and beauregard whips whare he is [in Tennessee] that will end the war. Allso the yankees say they wont fight any longer than June for they couldent stand the hot wether an they are a bout to starve. . . .

"Thomas I would like to no how you like to wash by this time or whether you wash your self or not. . . .

"I got up sick this morning with a bowl complaint and puking an sick at the stumack. I have not felt well all week but I thought I would not say any thing a bout that. . . .

"Your father tries to quarel with me a heep a times but I wont listen to him and he soon gets tired of quarling by his self. . . ."

Mrs. Fisher then closed with a poem: "I hope the

time will soon come / When the yankees the South may run / When you can come and see your sons three / And love and sleep with me."[13]

On March 23, Gen. "Stonewall" Jackson with a division-size force attacked Federals at Kernstown on the outskirts of Winchester. This was the opening engagement in a campaign for possession of the agriculturally rich Shenandoah Valley. In a 48-day period Jackson and his "foot cavalry," as his infantry were labelled, would march over 670 miles and win a half-dozen contests against three Union forces that outnumbered Jackson three to one at times.

Many of Jackson's early successes came from his cavalry chief, Col. Turner Ashby. A member of the 42nd Virginia wrote his mother midway through the campaign: "Ashby (Col. of a cavalry reg't.) is fighting their pickets and scouts almost every day. Col. Ashby is a useful man here in the Valley. He annoys the Enemy nearly to death, takes some prisoners and kills some nearly every day."[14]

Yet at the time the major focus in Virginia was the Tidewater region.

By the end of April, Gen. McClellan had transferred his 120,000 soldiers to the peninsula formed by the James and York Rivers. He planned a direct advance toward Richmond, the opponent's king in McClellan's chess game of war. The first opposition to the movement came May 5 at Williamsburg. Federals struck the rearguard of the smaller Confederate army. An all-day fight in the rain ended with Southerners falling back in the face of mounting odds.

"It was the first real battle" for most of the participants, a Richmond soldier noted. "I nearly emptied my cartridge box and judging by the number left, claimed in letters written home I had killed twenty nine Yankees but from experience gained in subsequent fights doubt whether I ever hit where I looked, but somebody must have aimed correctly as there were a great many dead yankees left on the field."[15]

McClellan's control of the lower end of the peninsula extended to Norfolk, the state's principal seaport. Proud citizens found themselves under martial law. "A melancholy Sabbath, not a churchbell has been heard this day," Camilla Loyall wrote the first day of Norfolk's occupation. "The whole city alive with Yankees. Many are afraid to go in the streets; the harbor crowded with vessels of every description; the Union flag floats from all the public buildings; a day of deep humiliation to the whole city. We are entirely cut off from the Southern Confederacy."[16]

Southern morale jumped upward with news later in May that Jackson's artillery and cavalry had broken the Union line at Winchester. The Confederate general had driven his men to the outskirts of the key city in the lower Valley. At dawn on May 25, Cpl. Marshall Frantz stated that the Southerners remained in line "at least an hour while Ball, shell, canister, grape and minnie balls were showered over our heads as thick as hail, but through the protection of Divine Providence few of us were hurt."

Then Jackson unleashed his infantry, which overran the make-do Union lines. "On they went," Frantz continued, "Helter-Skelter, Hurry, scurry, & we right after them. Our advance fought them right in the streets of Winchester and took a good many prisoners. After pursuing them 4 miles this side of Winchester we took up camp about 12 O'clock as our men were completely broke down. . . . The Yankees seemed to be scared to death."[17]

Some Union soldiers admitted being overwhelmed. One was Daniel Brown of the 2nd Massachusetts. "I felt like giving up and letting the rebels have me if they wanted but the thought of, how will Father & Mother feel when they know it? made me go on and on till I got clear to the Potomac river."[18]

Meanwhile, Union forces struggled through rain and mud to within nine miles of the Confederate capital. The swollen Chickahominy River split the Federal host into two parts. On May 31, Confederates attacked one wing at Seven Pines. Cumberland County soldier William Moss wrote: "Oh it was the most horrible fight that any one ever experienced. . . . We had to wade through mud and water above our knees. . . . I cannot tell whether I killed any one or not, but I shot often enough."[19]

George Newlon of the 8th Virginia agreed that Seven Pines was "as har[d] fighting as have ever been done." He added: "Our troops charged the yankees out of thire breast works and fallen timber. a company [of] the sixth Alabama regiment lost 27 men killed in [the] space of twenty yards square but they made the yankees run like sheep."[20] Newlon failed to say that the Federal army took advantage of strategic mistakes by Confederate generals, regrouped, and drove the Southerners back to their original position.

For those who survived their first engagement, the human debris of battle was repulsive. Artilleryman Wyatt Akers from Montgomery County wrote shortly after Seven Pines: "I went down towards the battle ground about a mile: evry house is full of wounded men. . . . It would raise the hair on any man's head to see the wounded and hear the groans. I was present when they commenced cutting off one man's leg but I had to leave. I could not stand and see the performance."[21]

Rumors always filled the after-battle lull. Robert Haile of the 55th Virginia heard that 300 of 400 Essex County men in his regiment had been lost in the fighting. "I am very sorry that such reports should get out," Haile wrote, "it causes a great deal of uneasiness to those who have ones who are near and dear to them in our regiment."[22] Haile died July 26 in Richmond from a paralyzing bullet wound.

The wounding at Seven Pines of Gen. Joseph Johnston led to the appointment of Gen. Robert E. Lee to head the Confederacy's premier army. As Lee secretly laid plans for a full-scale counterattack, spirits in Richmond received electrifying news. In mid-June a cavalryman stationed in Charlottesville speculated: "Jackson and his army is still on the march. No one knows exactly where he is."[23] Then came confirmed reports that Jackson had defeated the Union forces and regained control of the indispensable Valley of Virginia.

It was an extraordinary feat, performed by extraordinary soldiers. One of them, Robert C. Brown of the 4th Virginia, wrote his sister of one segment of the campaign. "Last weeke they like to march me to death. They march us six day[s]. Dident eat but four times in six days. . . . I broke down in win chester. The ambulance was behind. I cralled in that an road six miles" before resuming the march. After twin victories at Cross Keys and Port Republic ended the campaign, David R. Willis of the same regiment stated: "I do not no how long [we] will stay here but not long. I recon Old Jack cant go longer than two days without a fight."[24]

On June 26, Lee launched a series of attacks designed to drive McClellan off the peninsula. Each of five battles seemed to become progressively worse as McClellan retired slowly toward the James River and the heavy guns of anchored warships. All-day fighting occurred June 30 at Glendale. That night Maj. Henry DeShields assisted men in bringing off several captured Union cannon. "It was a heavy awkward job," the major stated. "Eight horses lay dead & dying around each piece. The night was dark and as we tried to extricate them from the strong artillery harness we would tread on the wounded & dying Yankees that had fought bravely at their guns. I shall never, never forget what a night of nights—the cries and groans of the wounded calling for water & for help—the anxious soldiers looking for their comrades—brother weeping over brother."[25]

The following day, Lee suffered clear defeat when his infantry columns charged up Malvern Hill against entrenched infantry and combined army-naval artillery. Howard Walthall of the 1st Virginia visited the carnage the day after the one-sided contest. "Such a horrible sight I never thought I could live to describe. Men lay dead in long rows where one of those enormous [gunboat] shells had ploughed through the ranks and slain them by scores and hundreds, mutilating them in the most awful manner, rows of them with top[s] of the head blown off and the half skulls like goards full of rain water. . . . The noise of those shells ploughing through the air was fearfully terryfying. Going through a body of woods they sounded like a train of cars."[26]

Heavy casualties notwithstanding, Lee had hurled back the first major threat on Richmond. Jackson stood unchallenged in the Valley. "This was the bright time of the Confederacy," Mrs. Elizabeth Callender of Prince George County recalled.[27]

Across the way, however, an equally positive mood dwelled among Union soldiers. New Yorker Frederick Watkins reassured his mother, "Though our rapid movements and hard fighting has been very severe and telling on the men, our confidence in Gen. McClellan is undiminished, and our hopes of a victorious termination of the war as bright as ever."[28]

Massachusetts artilleryman Lewis Holt, assigned to one of the batteries in the Washington defenses, stated after hearing news of McClellan's retreat: "The folks at home who talk of guiveing up must either be fools or crazy. I dont see any thing to be discouraged at and even if I did, if the rebels were to drive us from the paninsula guiveing up would be the last thing to be thought of. The only way to do is to start again with new strength and moore detirmination to concor at all hazards let the cost be what it will."[29]

Federals continued to trample upon parts of the state. On the Eastern Shore, Gen. Henry Lockwood illegally seized the home and furnishings of Dr. George Kerr for a Union headquarters. Lockwood also and arbitrarily declared the physician's slaves henceforth to be "freemen."[30] In Warrenton, Betty Gray noted bitterly: "For five days Abraham's troops have been sauntering to our door in groups. Yes, we have seen

Member of a prominent Bedford County family, Peter Lee Huddleston (1837–1923) served as a lieutenant in the 28th Virginia. Upon losing his commission in the 1862 regimental elections, he transferred to the 2nd Virginia Cavalry for the remainder of his service.

the Yankees to perfection in all varieties from horse stealer to hen roost robber & penetentiary men. Just caught two in the hen house."[31]

Much of Virginia's landscape already bore the scars of war. Lieutenant Gaines wrote his wife from Gordonsville, "Between the Armies of Genl Johnston last winter & spring & Genl Jackson this summer the whole country from this to Richmond is pretty well eaten out."[32]

Soldiers sweltered in a summer that was long and unusually hot. "It is regular dog day weather here now," Warren Holt of a Massachusetts battery told his sister. "The tents are black with flies in the day and the air is full of musquetoes at night." The same writer added a couple of weeks later: "The attractions of camp life are not great but then we get used to it. You know they say every body has got to eat a peck of dirt. Well I believe I have got through with my Peck and commenced on somebody else."[33]

Religious revivals began appearing in Lee's Army of Northern Virginia. "A meeting commenced in our brigade yesterday," Charles Lasley of the 21st North Carolina wrote his father. "I hope that we will have a good meeting. There is a good deal of interest taken. There are a number of penitants, and I know that we would have a good time if we had more assistance. . . . I wish our regiment had a Chaplain."[34]

Marshall Frantz of the 42nd Virginia also longed for religious services. To his sister he confided: "Sometimes on Sunday when we hardly know it is Sunday here I can picture you all off in my mind. . . . You all are fixing to go to preaching. There is Pappy dressed up with his shoes off sitting in his shirt sleeves reading and Ma telling Ange what to get for dinner, you dressing Marty and Charlie and Emory hollering after you and saying '*doggone it, Jude, where's my shirt.*' Yes I see you and wish . . . I could be with you; but under the present circumstances I couldn't content myself. No I couldn't be hired to stay at Home when the sacred soil of my *native State* is invaded by a *merciless foe.*"[35]

In mid-July, Gen. John Pope led a newly created Federal army into the north-central Piedmont region. The bombastic Pope issued a series of threats to Virginia residents. Federal soldiers would confiscate property and live off the land; citizens would be held responsible for any guerrilla attacks on Union installations; anyone who aided Confederate soldiers would be regarded as spies and executed without benefit of trial.[36]

A Fauquier County diarist became livid. "This order has caused more distress & excitement than any before issued. Numbers of harmless Citizens are now hid in the mountains to escape the grasp of that celebrated old Scamp. . . . Justice will meet the bundle of self-conceit & Bragadocio ere it sees its end, & put old Pope as low as his boodog."[37]

Pope did not have time to carry out his threats. On August 9, at Cedar Mountain near Culpeper, "Stonewall" Jackson attacked the lead elements of the Union army. The battle was fought in 98-degree temperature. Men fainted from heat alongside those who fell from wounds.[38]

Jackson's assault stopped Pope's offensive. Lee shifted the remainder of his army to link with Jackson. The climax of the movement came August 28–31 in the battle of Second Manassas. It was the bloodiest struggle the war had yet seen. One summation of the engagement came from Lt. Henry Cranford of the 14th New York. "Since I wrote you last I have been through a *terrible ordeal*, but *thank God* I have come out of it *safe* & *unhurt*. . . . During ten days, we were eight under fire & fighting the enemy. On the 30th we had the final struggle & I regret to say, were defeated. The loss of life has been terrible. Out of our Brigade, we have lost 910, nearly half the men in the Brigade."

Three bullets passed through Cranford's clothing. "Our soldiers . . . fought like tigers, although mown down like grass, but [our defeat] was owing to lack of generalship in our leaders. Gen. Pope has proved himself a failure, ditto [Gen. Irvin] McDowell. . . . We are now just where we started from five months ago. Our National horizon looks dark & gloomy."[39]

Second Manassas was the campaign in which Robert E. Lee emerged as a superb field commander. In 90 days, he had turned the Civil War in Virginia from the Union threatening Richmond to Confederates threatening Washington. "Old Virginia is once more relieved from thraldom & oppression," an officer proudly informed his wife.[40]

Lee then determined to carry the war into the North. A bold advance, with victory on Northern soil, might lead to demands for peace from disgruntled Unionists. During September 4–7, the Confederate army waded across the Potomac at fords in the Leesburg area. "The scene was most beautiful & imposing," Charlotte County soldier Richard Gaines wrote as he watched Jackson's division move in two columns across the wide stream. "The river, the valley on either side and the adjacent hills, were covered with troops and every thing else which pertains to an army, and the boys made the welkin ring with hussas and songs of Maryland, My Maryland. . . . We pushed on without halting to attend to the calls of nature and reached this point [Frederick, Maryland] at 9 o'clock P.M."[41]

The Potomac crossing was not done pain-free. John Griggs, an Essex County resident serving in the 55th Virginia, stated, "I dont believe there are two men in the Regt that has not blistered feet and a good many are bare footed but have to march."[42]

Lee also had a health problem. A day before the river crossing, he fell while mounting his horse and sprained both hands. He entered Maryland at a critical moment "riding in an ambulance, his right arm in a sling."[43] In that impaired condition, Lee led his army through the bloodiest one-day battle in American history.

Scores of volumes have been written of the battle of Antietam Creek. Lieutenant Richard Gaines witnessed only the first third of the fighting. Nevertheless, his account gives a strong sense of the intensity and emotion of that September 17 struggle.

"At the crack of dawn they commenced pouring down the mountains with this immense rable horde & assaulted our men with the fury of desperation and the malignity of devils. . . . Their first object was to drive us down between the mountains & the Potomac upon Harpers Ferry, and crush Genl Lee . . . but this able Genl & wily old fox [Jackson] was just on our left when in the morning they made this terrible assault. The veterans of Jackson not only stood their ground but drove them back a mile almost turning their right flank. But in this dreadful conflict his [Confederate] army was almost annihilated. In some regiments & companies hardly a man is left to tell the tale. . . .

"Not more than one hundred [in the brigade] could be mustered this morning. . . . I hear of but two field officers left in it. . . .

"The fight continued til seven & 1/2 oclock in the night, making fourteen hours of continuous fighting. For length of time, numbers engaged, and casualties, no conflict of the war will compare with this. I cannot estimate the loss on either side. It is immense."[44]

Autumn came, and it was a "down time" for most Virginians. Lee's army needed complete reorganization. Lieutenant Gaines of the Staunton Hill Artillery explained why. "In one word our *resources are too limited*. We want subsistance, transportation, clothing, men, in fact . . . the absolute necessaries of a soldier. If you could see them in their present ragged, dirty & Lousy condition; many without hats, blankets & shoes, you would wonder how so much has been accomplished."[45]

Civilians under Union rule in northern Virginia found life more trying. Betty Gray declared that the privations being endured by those living around Warrenton "were never dreamed of before. Entirely surrounded as we are by this lawless [Union] army . . . we may be robbed of all we have. The produce that has been saved by the farmers . . . is now being carried off by the Blue Rogues or Red necks. . . . Gangs from 8 to 18 are constantly stalking up to our barn-yard to steal the poultry while another cluster are in the woods shooting our fat shoats."[46]

Late in September, Federal general John Dix submitted a report of conditions in the Norfolk-Portsmouth area. Prices and unemployment were high, critical items "not to be had at any price." The Union officer concluded: "The state of things is deplorable. The people are suffering for want of almost all the necessaries of life."[47]

Stagnation of camp life and lowering temperatures triggered new outbreaks of sickness. At the time of Dix's letter, soldier John Stone of Henry County wrote his wife: "Bad coles is very commond here. A good many people has got the fever & chills."[48]

The same was true on the Federal side; and while medications were more numerous and plentiful, finding a cure could be troublesome. Freeman Colby of the 39th Massachusetts spent a month fighting a cold, only to contract jaundice in late autumn. "I never want to have the jaundice again," he told his parents. "The Surgeon gave me 10 Blue pills, one each morning in succession & a dose of salts at night to carry it off. Besides I have taken quinine enough to kill a Reg. . . . But I have got a disease a damn sight worse than jaundice on me now. I have laid here with the sick untill I am all covered with body lice as big as young calves and I am afraid they will either carry me off or carry my clothes off & leave me without any."[49]

Rarely was news from home of a positive nature. Some messages ripped at the heart. On September 28, just after Lee's army recrossed the Potomac, Bedford County wife Nancy Franklin informed her husband in the 2nd Virginia Cavalry of the deaths of their infant daughter and newborn son. "All that comforts me any," she declared, "is I believe their sufferings are at an end. . . . I would have given the whole world if possible if you could have been here and if you could but come now it would be a great consolation to me. . . . I dont see how I am to keep house I am so lonesome."[50]

Thomas Fisher of the 51st Virginia got even more crushing news two days later. "My Dear husband I will endever to right you a few lines for perhaps it may be the last riting you will ever see from me. . . . I got up monday morning and I could jest feel that my throat was sore and before night I could hardly swallow. And today I feel that I am not long for this world: the diptheria or some thing has got in my belly. . . . Oh if I die what will become of my little babies."

Frances Fisher then composed a 16-line poem that ends: "oh babe try and come home / And with me these hills roam / oh what a pleasure it would be / To talk and bee with thee."[51]

Union general George McClellan was a perfectionist, which meant that he was never quite ready to fight a battle. He had stopped Lee's advance at Antietam Creek, but his repeated failure to follow up the success exhausted even Lincoln's patience. On November 7, the president fired the most popular general the Army of the Potomac ever had.

Billy Yanks stationed in Virginia were almost unanimous in their anger at the action. New Yorker Henry Cranford, obviously not in tune with the Republican administration, wrote home: "The *infernal dogs of fanaticism* have never let up until they have succeeded in removing McClellan, the man in whom *we all* (the *army*) have placed our *faith* & *trust*. . . . It has caused a universal groan throughout the army. . . . I begin to fear that it will take a long time to crush out this rebellion, if we ever do."[52]

The new army commander, Ambrose Burnside, knew that he was expected to take the offensive promptly. He devised a simple but promising plan: to shift the Union army swiftly and secretly to the east, cross the Rappahannock River at Fredericksburg, and turn Lee's flank away from Richmond.

At first the strategy succeeded. The Army of the Potomac got the jump on Lee's forces and marched undetected through rain and mud. "I havent the least idea what is to be done," Massachusetts soldier David Hicks admitted. Artillery teams were strained to the limit by the weather. Frederick Watkins of the 4th New York Light Artillery noted, "The horses were wild for want of food and one man had his nose bit nearly off by one of his horses as he went to give him his oats."[53]

Pontoon bridges were to be waiting at Fredericksburg for the move over the Rappahannock. Administrative red tape delayed their arrival for a month. By then, Lee's army stood massed in earthworks on high ground immediately behind the town. Getting around the Confederate army was now impracticable. So Burnside determined to deliver major head-on assaults and fight his way through Lee's position.

First, Union artillery blasted Fredericksburg at point-blank range. (One six-gun battery fired 1,200 rounds on a single day.[54]) Then Union columns started forward. Thirteen times they attacked; thirteen times the ranks were shot to pieces.

A Massachusetts soldier wrote home: "Our army crossed over the river on to a plain which was surrounded by hills which the enemy held. We attacked along the whole line the next day with uniform results: repulsed at all points. . . . We gained nothing. . . . The result of this battle is the loss of 15,000 men killed and wounded and the knowledge that the enemy has quite as large an army as our own."[55]

A member of the 30th Virginia expressed the view: "This is a scene that ought to fill every heart with solemnity. How many poor souls have gone to their final home from the battle-field that stretches out before us! . . . If this scene fails to teach a man that his life is a vapor, and frail as the flower, what can do it?"[56]

Christmas found the two great hosts staring menacingly at one another with only the Rappahannock separating them. Sergeant Alexander Seiders of the 151st Pennsylvania spoke for thousands when he wrote, "I thoght of them that was home that Chrismas morning, what good things thay would have to eat but it [passed] over with out another thought."[57]

When 1862 began, the majority of Northerners had believed in a quick victory and a restored union. Now, at year's end, it was obvious that the Civil War was going to be long, bloody, and costly. To have peace, one side would have to conquer and the other side be conquered.

1863
"Our Loss Was Far Greater"

On New Year's Day, from her ancestral home near Warrenton, the usually despondent Betty Gray searched for confidence. "There is no happy faces today. . . . In the last twelve months how many sad tears have been shed? . . . But still that bright essential part of our frail existance has not entirely been crushed out. Dark as the clouds may appear, there is hope for a brighter day."[1]

Discontent coursed through the ranks of Union soldiers following defeat at Fredericksburg and the weeks of inactivity thereafter. Massachusetts artilleryman Lewis Holt explained why. "The army of the Potomac is lying idle as usual. They dont seem to accomplish any thing and I dont think they ever will till they [get] a new set of officers. I think that a great potion of their officers are rebels at heart just as much as Jeff Davis is and we never can expect to be victorious as long as we have such men to lead our men. . . . Day before yesterday . . . there was twenty one Major Generals in the city of Washington besides Brigadiers and other officers without number. No wonder the army dont do any thing."[2]

Ill-fated General Burnside then attempted another flank march around the Confederates. "I dont relish the idea of a winter campaign much," Private Hicks of the 13th

Massachusetts wrote. "It will be a tough one."³

Mother Nature made it so. Rain and sleet reduced Burnside's army to a mob struggling over land that had no bottom. A week into the campaign, a Union staff officer reported from Belle Plain: "But next morning we learned that the artillery, pontoons & wagon trains were all stuck in the mud some miles back. In the first place we could not cross [the Rappahannock] without the pontoons & in the next place we could not fight without artillery & thirdly we could not survive without subsistence. It was a deadlock. We layed there all day. . . . It was decided that the next morning we should all start back for our old camps, which we did . . . but all was ruin. . . . Our tents did not arrive till late last night."⁴

The "Mud March" finished Burnside as an army commander. His successor was "the sanguine, sagacious" Joseph Hooker. To fellow New England soldier David Hicks, "Fighting Joe" was the long-sought hero. "He is tall, a little angular in his frame. Sits [on] his horse with very square shoulders. His complection is florid; his eye is very pleasant and looks as though he would as soon speak to a private as a General. . . . He will prove the greatest general in the country and in the world."⁵

Various activities filled the winter army encampments. Adequate supplies depended on where a regiment was stationed. From camp near "Moss Neck" in Caroline County, Matthew Wells of the 21st Virginia told his father: "Only hard times and worse A coming I am fraid. We get About half A nuff to eat and nothing to drink and Aplenty duty to do."⁶ Yet Major DeShields in the 40th Virginia wrote home: "The men look fine—*well clothed, well fed* & with plenty of picketing to keep them busy. . . . We have visitors from the N[orthern] Neck nearly every day. They bring up all sorts of good things to the men—oysters abound!"⁷

A few days later, the same officer informed his wife: "It would do your very heart good could you sit in my tent this snow bright morning and listen to our boys—such snow balling & such shouting. . . . Every man seems as cheerful & well as possible."[8]

Johnny Rebs and Billy Yanks possessed more inherent similarities than differences. They had an identical background, common traditions and language, the same Christian faith, same hopes for the future. They could hate each other from a distance, but it often was difficult to be hostile at short range. In mid-January, Henry Puckett of the 42nd Virginia informed his family from the Rappahannock line: "The Yankeys is on one side of the river and our pickett is on the other. Our pickett Swap tobacco for coffee with them. They gave one plug of tobacco for too pounds of coffee. The order is that neither Side talk to the other but they will talk in Spite of order."[9]

Numbers of soldiers whiled away the winter months thinking of the fairer sex. The 51st Virginia's Burwell Hall, at the mountainous outpost of Narrows, determined to get married as soon as the war ended. "You wrote they was some of the girls seting their cap for me," he replied to a cousin. "That is good news to me. I intend to ketch one of them when I come home if I can. So you may tell them to look sharp for I am not a jokeing."[10]

And, of course, there were those who were battling sickness. David Hall, also at Narrows, informed his family in the Floyd County area: "The small pocks is still rageing hear. Tha is some five or six cases of them. . . . I expect it will be dangers to send leters if we all get it. I don't expect to write much till we get well. we mite giv them to you all."[11]

Hardships in turn brought homesickness. Major DeShields speculated about the town of his roots: "Heathsville must be a sad place. In its better days it was not by any means the busiest of little towns. . . . Still I feel that I would be willing to cast the anchor of my drifting bark there once more."[12]

Resumption of battle came with the springtime. General Hooker devised a strategy whereby he would divide his army and attack Lee simultaneously from west and east. Among Lee's talents as a field commander was his predictable ability to do the unpredictable. The Virginian split his own, smaller army into two parts to confront the dual threat. Then he split one wing again and sent "Stonewall" Jackson's divisions to strike the right, unprotected flank of the Union army.

"Old Jack's" assault came late in the afternoon of May 2. "It was first a murmur, generally increasing until like a gathering tempest," a member of the 61st Virginia remembered. The surprise attack overran the Union XI Corps. A federal artilleryman wrote that hundreds of Union troops "broke and ran away like a parcel of sheep."[13]

May 3 brought more intense fighting at Chancellorsville. The two sections of Lee's left united and slowly drove the Union army from fields and woods. Captain Murdaugh of the 61st Virginia recalled 15 years later: "The air was full of missiles; streams of shot and shell screamed and hissed on every side—it seemed as though nothing could live under that terrible fire—men and horses were torn limb from limb."[14]

Thick woods had been set afire by artillery shells; crackling flames mingled with thousands of voices that were a combination of the cheers of victors and the agonies of the wounded. Late in the action, Gen. Robert E. Lee "rode down the line accompanied by only an orderly. The soldiers held their breaths, expecting every moment to see him fall from his horse pierced by a dozen bullets, but still he rode on, while the shot roared and crashed around him. It was joy, all exulting joy."[15]

Chancellorsville was Lee's most resounding victory, but it came at terrible cost. On the night of May 2, with confusion everywhere, Gen. "Stonewall" Jackson was accidentally shot by his own men. He died of complications a week later. Crippling pain swept across Virginia. "Though lost to us, his name and Spirit still lives," a soldier from

Northumberland County declared. "Such universal and profound grief as is felt for Jackson was never felt for any one man before."[16]

Major William Pegram wrote his sister in Richmond: "There is quite a gloom over the army today, at the news of Jackson's death. We never knew how much we all loved him until he died." Near Warrenton, a saddened Betty Gray noted in her diary: "What a blast on our hopes. I can't realize our great loss. Brave Jackson, our Stone Wall, the Yankees' terror, our countrie's hero, gone."[17]

Five days of vicious combat in the Virginia Wilderness produced 30,000 casualties. Among the wounded Confederates was Ausbert Van Lear of Augusta County. Shortly after the battle he shocked his wife by writing: "I have now to inform you that I am badly wounded. I have lost my right leg. I was shot sideways through the knee and it was so badly shattered that I was obliged to have it taken off. . . . I am doing as well as could be expected. . . . I wish I knew you could come to see me."[18]

Optimism in the Union army had run high at the outset of the Chancellorsville campaign. A staff officer correctly analyzed where Hooker's strategy failed. "Hooker has proved himself *utterly incompetent*. . . . We had them whipped at every point & just at the moment when victory was ours, he got *frightened* & withdrew his army, very much against their inclination. . . . This has been the *grossest blunder* of the whole war."[19]

The post-battle lull gave some of its participants the opportunity to look at the "big picture" of the war in Virginia. Quartermaster DeShields felt a sense of frustration. Writing to his wife in Northumberland County, he thought it difficult for the Union army "to undertake to cross [the Rappahannock] again with his beaten host, but then they do really seem to be the most patient people on earth. It is a hard matter for us to teach them any sense though this army has exhausted most of its skill on them. Whipping them seems to do no earthly good."[20]

Both armies strengthened their ranks. This included executing a number of deserters to remind soldiers of the necessity of duty.[21] Troops awaited the course of action their commanders might take. Lee's cavalry chief, Gen. "Jeb" Stuart, assembled all of his mounted troops at Brandy Station and, with everything quiet on the front lines, staged a June 8 grand review. Charles McVicar of Chew's Battery watched the spectacle.

"As far as the eye can reach the cavalry are strung along in columns and a solid body. . . . There are several hundred ladies present to see us. A great many of them are riding in carriages or on horseback loping or cantering their horses around us in every direction. The staff officers are their knights. It is one of the most sublime scenes I ever witnessed. General Stuart and his body guard are riding over the ground reviewing us. There are several brass bands from Richmond playing at intervals from one end of the line to the other. The fair sex are seen on every side. The weather is clear and very pleasant.

"'Tis 4 o'c[lock], we are fighting a *Sham Battle*. The cavalry is charging across the field, the artillery is opening. The scene is beautiful beyond description."[22]

The next day, the Brandy Station parade ground was a battlefield.

Hooker was uncertain of Lee's intentions after Chancellorsville. The Union commander dispatched most of his cavalry to go out and search for Lee's position. On June 9, some 10,000 Federal horsemen charged into a like number of Stuart's men while they were encamped. The resultant fight was the largest cavalry action ever seen in the Western Hemisphere. All day opposing troopers fought—confused, wide-ranging, with riders charging, shooting, and hacking. Union cavalry left the field. For the first time, Federal horsemen had given as much as they got in a struggle with mounted Confederates.

Lee began a new offensive a few days later. To the Confederate general, the time seemed right to make a second raid into the North. A strong success on Union soil, following Hooker's defeat at Chancellorsville, might well create among Northerners a war-weariness that would end the struggle.

The Army of Northern Virginia got the jump on Hooker, moved around his western flank, and headed for the avenue of the lower Shenandoah Valley. Lieutenant John Minix of Page's Virginia Battery summarized the march in succinct but difficult spelling. "We left friedricksburg an marched to the valley of va. We run the yankeys away from beryville an run them from bunkers hill an from martonsburg an then to maryland. . . . We captured a great meny horses an guns an prisioners. Jineral uel [Richard S. Ewell] took too divisions an went by winchester an took nearly all of Jineral milroys [Robert H. Milroy's] army . . . an every thing he had an nearly all of his men. The vally of va is clear of yankeys now an Jineral lees army is falling into maryland an to pensylvania."[23]

Minix did not exaggerate in describing the rout of Milroy's large garrison at Winchester. A Massachusetts corporal wrote of the Union general reaching Harpers Ferry: "Towards night Milroy came in with his staff and about two hundred cavalry and said that . . . his whole command was retreating towards Harpers Ferry. . . . There was a good deal of hard talk here with the soldiers because he came in alone and left all of his infantry to shift for themselfs. . . . I do not think one half of his command ever got in here. . . . It was the greatest skedadle that ever I saw."[24]

Lee advanced steadily into Pennsylvania until the Union army—now under new commander George G. Meade—intercepted the Confederates at a vital crossroads named Gettysburg. The bloodiest battle of the war followed. Two days of combat raged in the rolling country and was a prelude to an assault Lee ordered on July 3 against the center of the Federal works. The 1st Virginia was dispersed as a picket line. Richmond's Howard Walthall never forgot the mammoth artillery duel that preceded Gen. George E. Pickett's assault with two divisions.

"Imagine the noise of four hundred canons firing at each other. It was terrific and with the rays of the sun was enough to weaken the bravery of the strongest. The shells were exploding over our heads and hurling death in the ranks. The two men on my right and left were struck. . . . I know I felt almost paralized and would have dug a hole in the ground to escape if it had been possible. . . . This firing was preliminary to an advance. When it ceased we were ordered forward. Rising on our feet we saw a great valley stretching out below and a peach orchard in full bloom. . . . As far as an individual could see, the army had gone all to pieces, cut all to pieces as the common expression went."[25]

The assault, known in history as "Pickett's Charge," lasted 40 minutes and added 7,000 more Confederates to the casualty lists. One of those who fell sent this message home to Buckingham County: "Dear Mother, I am here a prisoner of war & mortally wounded. I can live but a few hours more, at farthest. I was shot fifty yards of the enemy's line. They have been extremely kind to me. I have no doubt about the final result of this battle and I hope I may live long enough to hear the shout of victory, before I die. I am very weak. Do not grive my loss. I had hoped to have been spared but a righteous God has ordered otherwise & I feel prepared to trust my cause in his hands. Farewell to you all. Pray that God will receive my soul. Your unfortunate Son John."[26] The young soldier's remains lie somewhere near the Gettysburg battlefield.

To those who were there, Gettysburg was a defeat but not a decisive one. Major DeShields of the 40th Virginia told his mother rather haughtily: "In many respects our Campaign in Pa. is viewed by many as a disastrous one [but] although I believe we inflicted a much greater loss in *numbers* upon the enemy *our* loss was far greater. We lost *men* good true &

brave. They lost but so many beings who were the willing tools of a tyrant & a usurper. Our losses visited sorrow and bereavement to the homes & hearts of thousands whilst their losses only disposed of the cargoes of emigrant ships."[27]

From camp at Brandy Station, artilleryman Charles McVicar noted in his diary: "Lying on the review ground, a tired set. No rations yesterday or today. Most of the boys are asleep, some too tired to move, others are scouring the country for green apples. We are fighting for all we hold near and dear to us, not a murmur of discontent can be heard. . . . [This] Sunday is as any other day with hardships but Thank God we are willing that it should be too, rather than sacrifice our independence to a set of fanatical abolitionists."[28]

The surrender of Vicksburg, Mississippi, on July 4 opened the Western theater to Federal inroads and was regarded by Southerners as the more major setback. The fall of the river port, an Alabama soldier wrote from Dranesville, "has disheartened & discouraged every soldier in the army. I expect it will cause hundreds to desert."[29]

Most Virginians, locked in the counties where they lived, were ignorant of military affairs and thus victims of rumors and conjectures that followed any combat with the Federals. Nannie Bowie, living at Sandy Point in Westmoreland County, wrote another resident of the Northern Neck: "You can well imagine how extremely anxious we are to hear some tidings of our army. Yesterday we heard that Gen Lee was between Washington and Baltimore and intended attacking the latter place, that Hooker had been superceded & various other rumors, all of which we would like, but are afraid to believe. . . . I feel entirely cut off from the outer world, unable to hear or see anything that's going on elsewhere."[30]

With no Union pursuit after the Gettysburg disappointment, Lee's forces settled encamped in the northern Piedmont of Virginia. The army underwent not only reorganization by the officers but reevaluation by the enlisted men. "I think the trip to Pa. give our men & the yankees as much [fighting] as they want for awhile," Pvt. Christopher Crouch wrote from Orange. "If all the Regt. had lost like ours we would have been compeled to have given up the struggle. Ours was and offal loss. . . . I see no chance to stop the war. . . . The best news I have is to say we have had a grate revival of Religion in our Command, a grate many have been converted. . . . We desire the pray's of all *God* people to sustain us in the hour of temptation."[31]

A persistent thought among soldiers was that their next battle would end the war and permit them to come home. Andrew Graham's 51st Virginia was part of reinforcements sent to Lee. From Culpeper the Wythe County soldier wrote a cousin: "We will Stay here and rest a while if the yankees dount run us out from here. . . . I expect we will have to fight them in a few days. . . . Some thinks that this will be the desideing battle. I hope it will. The Southern men are runing a way So much that I believe it will brake our army. There has thirty nine of our Company runaway Since we got to Staunton."[32]

The Middlesex Artillery prepared defenses at Rapidan Station. John C. Clarke informed his sweetheart, Lizzie: "We are now in line of battle at this place, & expecting the yankees to advance every day. Our forces are buisily engaged in throwing up fortifications, and when they do come to give them h—l, to the tune of dixy. Excuse me my dear, for writing you such language."[33]

With letter writing the only form of communication in that day, the receipt—or lack of—news from home was a vital part of soldier life. John Cummins of the 27th Virginia demonstrated this in a strong rebuke to his brother in Rockbridge County. "I have received no letter since I went into Pennsylvania. Almost three months ago. Is it not a shame that I get no letters from home or friends while my comrades are getting letters almost daily. Does it not look like there was a coldness existing between us. . . . I hope you will do me the justice to answer this if received."³⁴

The quietness of autumn was momentarily broken on October 11, when the two sides had a sharp exchange of gunfire in Culpeper County. A Virginia artilleryman gave a gruesome description of part of the action. "A horrible sight here, our gun fired into a squad of videttes, one shell bursting among a group and got four horses and three men. The top of ones head was gone, part of one's spine and his bowels partly out. He begged us to give him some water and shoot him, to put him out of his misery. We gave him water but could not shoot them. One was bleeding to death from a piece of shell through his thigh."³⁵

Lee shifted his army to get between Meade's forces and the Northern capital. General A. P. Hill, commanding one of Lee's three corps and advancing with more alacrity than reconnaissance, sent Gen. Henry Heth with two divisions to attack what was thought to be the rear of the Army of the Potomac. At Bristoe Station, two Confederate brigades slammed into an entire, entrenched Federal corps. John Clarke of the 55th Virginia described part of the action: "We have been on the march for 10 or 12 days, after old Meade. We over took him on the plains of manassus, & our battalion suffered very much, 5 guns were lost . . . we lost 30 men killed & wounded & 43 horses. Our battery was not engaged in the fight. We were ordered off on another road on picket & so we did not get up in time. I consider that we were blessed."³⁶

Lee suffered 1,400 casualties—one man fell every two seconds of the contest. Union losses were less than half that number. A disgruntled Major DeShields told his wife: "The enemy went too fast for us. We overtook about 10,000 but by the mismanagement of A. P. Hill or Heth they slipped through our fingers *most disgracefully*. . . . I hope [they] will be displaced or superseded by abler men."³⁷

By late 1863, Richmond was a swollen metropolis of 300,000 people fighting against crowded housing, hunger, inflation, and attendant diseases. Prisoner of war compounds added to the discomforts. Mary Fontaine, daughter of one of the city's most prominent clergymen, wrote on November 10: "There are some 15,000 Yankee prisoners now in and around Richmond and I think with the small guard we have now it is really dangerous. A plan for breaking out on Bell Isle was discovered the other day and I don't know why they could not in a crowd get out and up to the armory before much could be done. If they do, who are safe here in the very midst of prisons?"

Fontaine then added: "The religious feeling in the city still is intense, churches crowded nightly with serious persons. We had a beautiful baptism on Sunday night—27 were baptised and Pa [John L. Burrows] was in his glory. Mr. Dandridge says he reminds him of a duck he is so fond of the water!"[38]

The Middlesex Artillery was on guard at Rapidan Station when unexpected visitors appeared. "Oh, I forgot to tell you," gunner John Clarke wrote his sweetheart. "We had the honour of a call by President Davis last week, escorted by Gen. Lee & staff. Oh, Gen. Lee is so much the finest looking of the two. We all give Uncle Jef. three cheers as he passed. The old Gentleman seem to be in fine spirits, and saluted us as he passed by the raising of his hat."[39]

Christmas Day found Betty Gray's family huddled alone in their Fauquier County home. Their slaves had all left voluntarily or impressed. "Bright & beautiful is the sun," Gray wrote in her diary, "but any thing like brightness contrasts so badly with our care worn & troubled hearts. . . . We never saw a Christmas without a party & pleasure untill this cruil war in its rage turned all pleasure into pain, all times of enjoyment in to grief & mourning. . . . Never after this shall I enjoy any thing like frolicking or dancing on this day."[40]

Quartermaster DeShields ended the year with an admission to his wife. "I must confess that I dont see the fun of it all. I'm tired of it. This is too long a stretch for me. I wouldn't be satisfied with anything now but a sight of precious family. I wouldn't give my wife & babies for the whole Confederate states with all its appurtenances & appendages—no not for one of your little fingers."[41]

1864
"This Cruel War"

George McSwain was 34 years old and did not want to go to war. He was quite content as a farmer with a wife, two children, and a small spread of land in the North Carolina Piedmont. Yet when a large contingent of Cleveland County friends enlisted in October 1861, McSwain felt compelled to do the same. He became a member of the 34th North Carolina.

Within nine months his wife, Hanna, was begging him to come home and see to the family's growing needs. McSwain deserted in July 1862 and remained at home until his voluntary March 1863 return to the army. A crisis of some sort prompted McSwain to rush back to his family a month later, again without official permission. He rejoined his regiment in November. On January 3, 1864, from camp at Orange, McSwain sent a letter to his family.

"It is with painful regret that I have to say to you in way of writing my last letter that I ever expect to write in this world to you, as my days are but few that I have to spend in this unfriendly world, as I expect to part this life on next Saturday by the sentence of a General courtmartial, to be tied down to a stake on that day, the 9th of this month, and be shot to death with musketry.

"But little thought I had of this when I volunteered in the service of my country, to protect my home and family, that my life would be taken by my own people simply for absenting myself from my post with the view of protecting my little helpless children and affectionate wife. . . . Hanna, I was in very good heart all the time and dident think they would shoot me until yesterday morning my sentance came and was read to me that I had to be shot next Saturday.

"It washed against me like the raging billows against a lonely rock in a sweeping storm; and I have carefully examined myself and I feel well assured that when I leave this world that I will be at rest; but Oh! my little children and affectionate wife—may the Lord fit and prepare them to meet me in heaven where there will be no more grief, no more pain, no more sorrow, no more trials, no more war, no more parting of husbands and wives, no more parting of parents and little children there; but to be at rest for ever.

"Hanna, dear wife and dear little children: I never expect to see you any more in this life; but my prayers are that you will meet me in heaven. Do the best you can and may God and his mercy rest and remain with you for ever. Dear wife dont grieve nor trouble after me for I feel that I am going to a better world and be at rest and then I wont be here for to be punished any longer.

"My afflictions have been severe and I feel that I will be better off. Tell all my friends farewell for me, and farewell dear wife, farewell dear children. Prepare to meet me in heaven.

"I will close by saying: God bless my wife and children for ever.

"Farewell."[1]

McSwain was executed on January 9 and buried in an unmarked grave.

Confederate army morale in those first months of 1864 was generally low. Lee's men were not losing skirmishes or territory, but neither were they improving their lot or making gains in the struggle. Further, they were trying to endure the winter in a vast wasteland. On January 31, Betty Gray noted in her diary: "Oh! the destruction the Enemy are depredating is too numerous to mention. Every vacant house in Warrenton & the vacinity, whenever the Tyrants can bear the sway have been brought low. In some instances where comfortable new dwellings stood their is not a vestage left to show their wantoness deeds. Auburn is entirely demolished."[2]

Inactivity in camp brought stagnation. This in turn generated dreams of war's end and a return home. From Orange County in January, Morris Whetzel of the 33rd Virginia announced to a cousin: "This is a hard life to serve. We are hard up for some thing to eat. . . . I think we will haf to go up the spout before long. We are a ruin set of Rebels. I am getting out of heart [with] this kind of life."[3]

Mecklenburg County soldier Thomas B. Jones wrote his brother-in-law the same month: "I am in the hopes the time will soon come when we may all meet around the fireside of our sweet old home that we did not know how to appreciate until this cruel war came and took us from them. . . . I am just trying to get out of this war. I am not thinking about the will for us as I don't think I will be setting about washing my shirts and killing lice."[4]

A few weeks later, Edgar Ashton of the 3rd Virginia told his family in Portsmouth: "There is not a day passes of my head but what I have thought about all of you and have often wished for this war to close so we could return to our homes and live together in peace, but do not see much prospect for it to come to a close for sometime yet to come. . . . No one knows the privations and hardships I have been through since I left home."[5]

Forty-three-year-old Sgt. Eli Coffelt was on duty that winter in the Shenandoah Valley with the 23rd Virginia Cavalry. Being older than most of his compatriots, Coffelt had deeper pains of homesickness. "I should like to be home verry much," the Shenandoah County native wrote his wife.

Child photograph, undated. Other than his wife, no individual evoked more feelings in a soldier than did his child. Family ties were extremely strong, in great part because life in mid-nineteenth-century America was simple and unencumbered by a flood of trivia.

"Since I last left home it seemes to go harder for me to stay away than ever. When I think of my dear wife an my four Dear children it sometimes almost breakes my heart to think that I should be seperated so far from them by this cruel war, but it seems that man is born to trubels as the sparks are to fly upwards."[6]

Abraham Lincoln once confessed, "I have often been driven to my knees by the realization that I had nowhere else to go." Many soldiers of the Civil War agreed with the Union president. Daniel Cox of Pittsylvania County stated to his parents: "We have [a] dark time in the future. . . . If the Lord does not fight for us we must be overcome. I think we all ought to humble ourselves, perhaps the Lord will look upon us. . . . God forbid that any of us should be cast away."[7]

Soldiers who visited Richmond early in 1864 were repelled by conditions in the Confederate capital. In one of his most scathing letters, Quartermaster DeShields asserted: "Richmond is the pride & the disgrace of the Confed. . . . Look at Richmond in its various aspects. It is the grandest, noblest, vilest, meanest, wickedest place in the Confederacy. There are here in her bosom the sublimest patriots around whose Spartan & Roman virtues are congealed all the hopes of the country. Many have censured the actions but who is there that has ever suspected the motives or doubted the virtues of our President (I'd take him for our *King*), and then there are those here, in high position too, whose well fed bodies cover lukewarm & traitorous hearts. There are vampires here who are preying upon the country's vitals whilst they chant the most approved paeans to her glory. Religion here I fear is eking out a shadowy existence."[8]

Offsetting such negativism to a degree was a sense of humor found to varying extent in every army camp. Just as spring began, Nathaniel Cleveland of the Fluvanna Artillery told his brother: "About 4 oclock [in the morning] the bugle was sounded for us to fall in & receive orders to move. Mess no. 1 did not go, but the most of the Co[mpany] fell in, &

then they were informed that it was an *April fool*. The Co. then pitched in & rode several of the men on a rail."⁹

Similarly, Middlesex's John Clarke veered from a camp report to a playful question for his fiancée. "Oh the log huts are scattered through the woods like wild varmints. I don't think I ever saw as many before, and so many girls, and some of them are really pretty & interesting. You must not be surprise if you hear of my falling in love with some of them. I think that I am intitled to 3 or 4. Cant you agree with me on this point? Well dearest one . . . I have no knews of interest to write you."[10]

By April, with temperatures rising and the mud drying, it was time again for battle. Confederates in Virginia were aware that there had been a change in the Union high command; yet the Southern army had handled the efforts of Gens. Irvin McDowell, George McClellan, Ambrose Burnside, Joseph Hooker, and George Meade with as much as each could handle. The announcement of a new commander of the Army of the Potomac created little anxiety in the Virginia encampments. Floyd County's David Hall reassured his cousin: "The generel report . . . says that old grant has gone to the east to take Richmond and I fear that he will get it because he has never bin whipped sens the war commens. But I think that General Lee can stand him a nuff on that."[11]

Edgar Ashton, of Portsmouth, was more optimistic. "I expect there will be hot work near Richmond this coming campaign if Grant makes an attempt to take the place which no doubt he will make one grand effort to do. I think some one will get hurt before it is taken, and if old Grant fools with Genl. Lee, he (Grant) will get himself in difficulty, for it just takes him (Lee) to set traps for such men as he is."[12]

Across the way, an unidentified Union soldier named William was encamped along the Rapidan River. As May began, he informed his brother: "Everything is kept very secret here. Gen. Grant dont divulge his plans and in this respect is very different from his predecessors. All I know is this, that a very great Army is concentrating in & about Culpeper. All the fields & heights, so far as I can see, is white with tents."

The Billy Yank continued: "We shall soon go from here, but *where*, I dont know. . . . But I am ready and I dont care how soon the campaign opens. It must come with all its dreadful realities and *waiting* is a torment. It is anything but pleasant to be in suspense. Therefore the sooner 'the ball' opens, the better I shall be pleased."[13]

The 1864 strategy of new Union general-in-chief Grant was the same simple pattern he had employed throughout the war: devise and try something. If it failed, attempt something else. Yet Grant's determination would never waver: he would hammer unrelentingly at the enemy, applying pressure until opposition collapsed. Grant told Lincoln that spring, "Whatever happens, there will be no turning back."

On Wednesday, May 4, an enormous Federal push began on several fronts. The main thrust, 120,000 soldiers in the Army of the Potomac, filed across the Rapidan on pontoons and headed into a wooded darkness known as the Wilderness. For the next 11 months (save for a brief interlude in June) the two opposing armies were never out of contact. It was a pounding, continuous campaign—the one type of war with which Lee could not cope. He could interfere with Grant's movements, but he could not impose plans of his own.

Fighting of some degree occurred almost daily. Tens of thousands of soldiers would fall across the Piedmont and through the Shenandoah Valley. It is called Grant's "Overland Campaign," and it would mark the sunset of the Confederacy.

Two days (May 5–6) of intense combat in burning woods were followed by two weeks of bloody engagements in and around Spotsylvania. One of Lee's couriers rode through the Wilderness a week after the fighting. "Many of the enemy lay unburied on the field," he noted. "Most of them were in an advanced state of decomposition and the stench was unbearable. In a pine wood where the enemy's dead marked their line of battle were trees perfectly riddled with musket balls; many trees being cut off by solid shot and shell. The marks of musket balls on the trees showed remarkably accurate firing, very few being higher than a man. Found in the Yank fortifications a great deal of plunder."[14]

War's destructive hand reached in many directions from the Wilderness/Spotsylvania site, and in some instances it extended over time.

Ann Hudson lived in Amherst County. Her husband was a member of the 49th Virginia. Two months after the major fight at Spotsylvania, Mrs. Hudson wrote her aunt in Nelson County: "Oh my Dear Aunt Jane what have I to tell you. Poor Shelton is dead. Oh the nearest & Dearest friend I had on earth is gone. He died 26 of June. He was wounded 12 of May. He got home in 2 weeks after he was wounded & I thought he soon would be well but oh he was taken so ill & suffered no tounge can tell & oh Aunt Jane he was so soon taken away from me. How can I bear it. I feell like one that dident have a friend one earth. May the lord have Mercy upon me & reconcile me to his Blessed will. . . . He is gone never to come back to me no more. How can I bear it, pray for me. It is all you can do."[15]

In mid-May, Surgeon George T. Stevens of the 76th New York arrived at Fredericksburg to attend the wounded from recent battles. Stevens recoiled at the sight. "The city is a vast hospital: churches, public buildings, private dwelling, stores, chambers, attics, basements, all full. There are thousands [lying] upon the sidewalks."[16]

Lee and Grant were locked in combat around Spotsylvania when another Union force, moving southwest to gain control of the Shenandoah Valley, met disaster at the battle of New Market. A member of Chew's Battery summarized the action: "Battle opened at 8:30 AM, Breckinridge in command drove the enemy through town to Rude's Hill. Here they made a determined stand. The line being a good one, the elevation in their favor, the [Virginia Military Institute] cadets made a splendid charge and never wavered. From the number of Blue dead and wounded, we showed admirable work, worthy of future history."[17]

Unusual acts of compassion occurred a week after the New Market struggle. Eight officers from Massachusetts and Pennsylvania issued a statement to be presented to other Federals invading the Valley.

"We the undersigned, officers of the Union army, now prisoners in the Confederate lines, desire to state for ourselves and the unfortunate wounded men who were left in the hands of the Confederates in the late battle near this place, May 15th, that we have received the kindest attention and every care possible from [Jessie] Rupert & Lady, F[erdinand] Zeiler & Family, Rev. J[acob] L. Stirewalt and Lady. That they have taken our wounded to their houses and have fed them from their private stores. That they have sought out our wounded in barns, outhouses, or where ever the fortunes of war left them and have labored assiduously to ameliorate their sufferings.

"We know them not only to be kind to us themselves, but that they have interested other friends in our behalf and that they are responsible persons whose word may be relied upon and whose property and rights ought to be sacred to every Union soldier."[18]

In another sector of Virginia, Union forces were stunted when, on May 16, Confederates under Gen. P. G. T. Beauregard attacked another enemy force at Drewry's Bluff. "A fierce fight ensued," the 1st Virginia's Howard Walthall wrote. "I . . . couldn't tell how we flanked the Yanks but I knew by the hastily erected log breastworks that we had gotten where they intended to meet us, for all along where we were there were great kettles of coffee hanging over fires, showing they were at breakfast when we surprised them and the firing began in reversed positions. The woods were dense and we couldn't see very far but we were behind their breastworks and had to stand up to shoot. Some men are more reckless than others and not so ready to take advantage of intervening obstacles. My brother Ryland of Co. G was one of that kind. I remember pleading with him not to expose himself so needlessly but he was a brave boy and full of spirit and excitement and was standing and shouting to the Yanks to come on when a ball crashed through his brain and he fell fluttering in my arms."

Walthall bore his brother's remains to the rear. He returned to the field to find his company "behind a clay bank on the river side. It had just passed through an awful shelling experience from gun boats in the river. The men looked like imbeciles. They had been under this shelling several hours which deafened them and the explosions covered them with the yellow dirt."[19]

The farther south Grant pushed his army, the nastier the fighting seemed to become. Union soldier Freeman Colby reported that oftentimes the troops fought an all-day engagement with empty stomachs, while the 13th Virginia's George Q. Peyton noted, "Our rations have been mainly corn meal and bacon—just eat it raw." As for water, Peyton added, all "we get is out of the puddles the rain leaves."[20] That Virginia was then undergoing a drought intensified the misery.

An unwell Robert E. Lee rode in a carriage as the two armies grappled along the North Anna River. The 51st Virginia was guarding Hanover Junction, but Pvt. David Hall could hear the roar of guns in the distance. He wrote home on May 26: "I hope that tha all will quit this foolishness be four we all get kiled but I hope that [God] will hav mercy on us all. I dont think that grant can ever Whip us hear. We ar well forty fied a ganst him. it is imposebl for him to charg our brest works."[21]

The heavy fighting also took a toll among civilians caught in the middle. Late in May, Helen Green Stewart

Howard Malcolm Walthall (left) and Robert Ryland Walthall were apparently twin brothers born in 1841. The two enlisted April 21, 1861, in the 1st Virginia. Howard was briefly a prisoner of war and was paroled April 15, 1865, at Lynchburg. Robert was wounded at Gettysburg before being killed in action May 16, 1864, at Drewry's Bluff.

of Todd's Tavern in Spotsylvania County made an appeal to a brother behind the lines. "We had a most terrific fight all around. The Yankey canons were planted on three sides of the hous. We did escape most wonderfully being struck by the balls. We never quit the hous, they made this their hospital. They burned all of our fense an took your hors and ours, every hog and left us but three sheep. They came in so unexpectedly we had no time to think. Indeed had we of known it I had no one to take them out of the way Stewart being sick at the time. . . . I could not tell you half my trials. They were great but enough. . . .

"I am thiner than I ever was. . . . Tell me if there is any chance for a body to buy something to eat up there. Down here there is nothing that can be had for love or money. The people must inevitably starve and we among the number. I can see no other alternative."[22]

Grant continued trying to outflank Lee and drive the Confederate army away from Richmond. The Southern commander would quickly shift his forces and block the move, even though after each engagement Grant drew closer to Richmond. When only five miles from the capital, Grant momentarily lost his patience and ordered a frontal attack against the works of one of the Civil War's most brilliant fortifications engineers.

Lee was ready on June 3 when Union columns rushed through piney woodlands and across open fields. George Peyton of the 13th Virginia recalled: "In the morning a perfect hurricane of musketry and cannon fire started on the right at Cold Harbor. The enemy charged our lines a great many times but was repulsed with great slaughter. For several hours the artillery fire was the heaviest and loudest I ever heard. . . . Our entire line was shelled during the day and pandemonium burst and inmates were running wild in Hanover."[23]

Some 7,000 Federals were killed or wounded while Lee's casualties were less than 1,500 men. Two weeks after the one-sided slaughter, a member of Chew's Horse Artillery rode over the terrain. "As we neared the fortifications what a horrible sight. Had to move ten or twelve bodies. Hogs had routed them into the road. The stench is so fearful, the horses will hardly pass. Our finer feelings are blunted. We hear jokes over this awful scene of bodies, piled here eight and ten deep as far along these breastworks as we can see. This is the most horrible catastrophic scene of wantonness or dreadful disaster. It scarcely calls forth a remark."[24]

Captain Joseph Halsey of the 6th Virginia Cavalry was on duty in Orange County during the Wilderness–Cold Harbor fighting. Ignoring the heavy losses suffered by the Confederate army, the officer sought to reassure his wife. "Three years ago we were alarmed at the idea of the Yankees raising 75,000 men to crush the rebellion. Within the last 4 weeks our Army under Lee has taken from Grant's forces fully that number & will destroy him utterly if he persists in running upon our breastworks manned by veteran troops. Disease too will soon begin its ravages in the peninsular swamps & bad water will do as much as a Minnie ball for our deliverance."[25]

Another captain, Henry Cranford of New York, agreed. "I do not think that this Campaign has been conducted with all the skill that it has had credit for. I think we might have gained (by a different programme) the position we now occupy, without such a terrible loss of life & limb, but Gen Grant fights on the Bull Dog plan. He has indomitable perserverence & will stick to it as long as he has a man left. Therefore the inference is that if the Govt. only fill up his losses as fast as he makes them, he will ultimately win. But you need not look for the downfall of Richmond for some time to come, nor until a great deal more blood is spilled. I would to God it were over."[26]

Not all Confederate soldiers were elated over the Cold Harbor massacre. The 13th Virginia was in reserve near Richmond during the major fighting. Charles Peyton of that regiment never forgot the disgust he felt at the inattention of the government to the needs of soldiers and civilians alike. "Our brigade gave one day's rations to the poor of Richmond," he wrote after the war. "But if rags, bare feet, hunger and no money indicate poverty, this army is the poorest set this side [of] eternity. . . . I don't suppose there was ever an attempt to set up an independent government with as many incompetent people in it as are in the Confederate Government at Richmond. My recollection is that they only paid off the army once in 1864 and all they had to do was to print the notes to do it with. No wonder it failed!"[27]

While Grant commanded Lee's attention, Gen. Philip Sheridan and 12,000 Union cavalry embarked on a raid against Richmond. The capital was never seriously threatened, but mounted Federals left destruction wherever they went. Louise Carter of Shirley Plantation in the lower peninsula unconsciously showed the transition in the struggle to total warfare when she wrote: "At this time, Sheridan raided through this country destroying every house in his track. The guard here saw the flame of brother Charlie's house and rode up there in time to put out the fire under the barn and quarters and stable. Dr. Turner's, Mr. Crenshaw's, Brother Charlie's and Riverside houses were laid low. If McClellan had been up here, he would never have allowed this destruction. He sent [Col.] Alfred Pleasanton (who was his Chief of Staff) up here three times to see if we needed anything or required assistance. Both had graduated in the [West Point] class with my brother George and were very good to us, but McClellan was a gentleman and, therefore, Lincoln did not care for his methods of warfare and had him removed."[28]

Sheridan's raid came at high cost. He lost some 1,500 troopers and almost that number of horses before reaching the safety of the Federal lines—and many of those losses came from Mother Nature. A Confederate cavalryman declared: "The weather is extremely hot, and dry. I do not think we have had a shower for a month, and the dust is terrible. Our

Cavalry is quite jaded, and many horses are broken down."[29]

In mid-June, Grant stole a march on Lee, skillfully shifted his army to the south side of the James River, and made for Petersburg, a railroad junction that was "the underbelly of Richmond." Lee barely managed to get his army in front of the city in time to prevent its fall. Both armies skirmished as each constructed earthworks. A soldier in the 39th Massachusetts told his parents: "There is now only a space of from 12 to 20 rods between the lines. . . . Though the lines are equally exposed the rebs cannot raise their heads above the works without receiving a shot, many of which prove fatal. . . . The two lines have been buried for over five days, & can only moove out of their trenches under cover of darkness for water or rations."[30]

One of those defenders was Charles Thomas of the 56th Virginia. "I don't like picket duty much," he confessed. "We have a very hot time sometimes firing at each other. . . . I gave them 20 rounds one night not long since and Robert give them 12. . . . The Pickets have stoped firing at each other but I don't like to trust them. They might crack a fellow. Our boys are very sickly. A great many have gorn to the horse pittle."[31]

Conditions were unpleasant as well with Confederate artillery units. Winchester's Charles McVicar wrote of his battery being in the saddle for eight days. "Have slept in old infantry camps, our clothes full of vermin as our wagons are back near Richmond. No change of clothes for two weeks past, officers and men scratching and not a few cuss words. We have never been filled with creepers for this long before."[32]

Initially, neither side envisioning a siege, each threatened extreme measures. Federal soldier Freeman Colby wrote late in June: "Yesterday the Rebs took a lot of our prisoners . . . into the city [Petersburg] so that we would not shell the place, & this morning Gen. Grant has ordered a retaliation by ordering us to place their officers now in our hands in front of our lines when we charge, so they will have to shoot their own officers in order to harm our line of battle. Better use honorable means & let Useless Grant alone."[33]

The two premier armies of the Civil War began preparations for what would be a nine-month standoff to the east of Richmond and Petersburg. Sergeant James Albright of the 12th Virginia Light Artillery informed the home folk: "The siege progresses slowly & no new developments are transpiring. Dig, dig, dig! is the word, while boom, boom, boom! from the mortars & the shrill whistle of the minnies, alone, break the monotony of the tiresome, demoralizing, debilitating siege."[34]

Federals celebrated the Fourth of July in an offensive manner, where Confederate soldiers were concerned. James B. Anderson of the 57th Virginia's "Pig River Grays" wrote in his journal: "The enemy, about eleven o'clock, told our picket to get in the pits. They were going to give a salute. Pretty soon they lumbered away with their canon rite at our lines. You ought to have seen the boys get to the works. It did not last long . . . I do not think [our] boys liked it, and not even as much as thanked them for their salute. In the place of thanking them for their salute, would have thanked them to have kept it to themselves."[35]

Living conditions in the Petersburg lines were awful from the start. After a month of such existence, the 57th Virginia's James Anderson stated: "It is got so hot that I can hardly hold my eyes open. The flies pesters me so I can not sleep for them."[36]

News from home was sporadic. Mecklenburg County's Charles Thomas complained that "we don't get no news only by [news]papers and they are generally filled up with lies."[37] On the other hand, Henry DeShields of Northumberland County was able to apprise his uprooted wife of conditions in their home area. "I have very little news from N[orthern] Neck, nothing from North[umberlan]d, but the Yankees have been in Westmoreland & Richmond Co[untie]s & acted terribly, most of them negro troops.

They were soon arrested in their exploits, however. Col [John Mercer] Brockenbrough got 3 or 4 hundred men together & fought them near Farnham church. Killed a number of them & started them to their gunboats flying & since then some 800 or 1000 men have been organized & armed for their own defense."[38]

Two days later, the same officer stated: "Grant I suppose will keep pegging away for some time to come but everybody feels confident that Genl Lee is doing all for the best. The whereabouts of Early is wrapped in much doubt—said to be at various points in Maryland but I have not the slightest idea where he is."[39]

General Jubal Early was, in fact, taking one of the great gambles of the war. He commanded what was left of "Stonewall" Jackson's old corps. In mid-June, after a Federal force under Gen. David Hunter burned and looted its way through the Valley to Lynchburg, Early's veterans first blocked and then sent Hunter's brigades fleeing toward the mountains. The aggressive Early then turned north and started boldly down the Shenandoah. His ultimate target was Washington, D. C.

The Confederates marched through Lexington on June 15. George Peyton of the 13th Virginia wrote: "When we got to the edge of town we 'reversed arms' and all the army passed by the grave of Stonewall Jackson who is buried in the cemetery there. The grave was a simple mound of earth with several wreaths of flower and evergreens on it. It had a tombstone over it but the Hunter thieves stole it and carried it off. They burned VMI and all buildings of a public character."

Peyton continued: "They hung Capt. White, a brother-in-law of Lt. [Conway] Newman of Co. A. They accused him of bushwhacking. Hunter ought to have been hung. We marched down the main street which was lined with pretty women and girls who had come to town to see the soldiers. If most of them looked as ragged as I did, they were hardly worth seeing!"[40]

Merchants in Frederick, Maryland, were just opening their shops on July 9 when Early's columns marched into town. "Some of our men got some hats and a few other things," Peyton admitted. "Old Jube levied a tax of $200,000 on the town and if they did not pay it, he said he would plunder it. They hustled around and borrowed the money from the banks and I do not think it was ever re-paid. They tried to make the U. S. pay it, but I do not think they did. Early gave this money to men to buy supplies for his army and a good part of it was kept by the people he gave it to."[41]

Lee hoped that the raid on Washington would force Grant to dispatch soldiers away from the Petersburg lines to protect the Northern capital. Grant did so; the arrival of two corps of Union veterans ended the threat to Washington. Union pressure below Richmond remained constant.

Early's feat gave a momentary lift to Confederate morale. The soldiers under Early boasted long and loudly at their accomplishment. Bristol's David Bailey recalled the 37th Virginia reaching Silver Spring, Maryland, and meeting an elderly woman fearful that the Southerners would burn down her home. "Madam," Bailey answered, "the General [who is lying up in an ambulance] is a little too drunk to see ladies, but he will shoot the first man that disturbs you."[42]

Southwest Virginia's Thomas Fisher cheerfully told his parents: "Our army went into Md. and went within 3 miles of Washington City which is closer than the yanks have been to Richmond this year. Our men brought out a fine lot of horses & cattle, destroyed many miles of Rail Road, busted up the Chesipeak & Ohio Canal, besides capturing and destroying vast quantities of army stores &c. This will ballance off with them for the Dublin & Lynchburg raids."[43]

Union soldiers tended to play down Early's campaign. Captain Henry Cranford wrote his wife in Brooklyn, New York, that "the Rebel raid . . . is looked upon as of very little consequence here, but nevertheless we have shipped off quite a number of troops to Washington to head them off. If the

A native of Charleston and born in 1843, George Baxter Hannah attended Virginia Military Institute before enlisting in the 14th Virginia Cavalry. Most of his duty was as a staff officer to General Albert Gallatin Jenkins (right). Hannah returned home after the war and lived until 1914.

home troops were worth a cent, this would not have been necessary."[44]

A half-hearted pursuit of Early's small army came to an abrupt halt when, on July 28, Confederates made a double envelopment of the Federals at the Battle of Second Kernstown. Thomas Fisher of Wythe County gave a rare, personal account of the action to his parents.

"The fight commenced about 10 oclock. I was in that fight . . . about 1 oclock Breckenridges old Division Comanded by Gen. [Gabriel] Whorton, was moved to the right, and came up on the enimies left flank. When all things were ready, the Rebble yell was raised all around the lines and we charged upon them; Gordens Division in their front and ours in their left flank. I was in the front rank, and had a fair view of the whole field. Nothing could be more grand (of that Kind) the Rebble ranks moved up steadily, without wavering accross fields, over fences & Ditches &c. The yankees stood for a while but as our line moved up, I observed their ranks began to waver. Soon they began to scatter, and broke accross the fields. Their Officers tried to keep them togeather, and in the mien time a yankee Officer came galloping accross the field in front of, & toward our regt. and kept beckoning with his sword for us to halt . . . when he got within about 75 yds we let off at him and killed his horse under him and wounded *him*.

"About a hundred yds further, and a regt of [William W.] Averills noted cavalry made a charge upon the head of our Regt. and the 45th. This looked somewhat scairy to see horsemen in full speed with drawn sabres comeing right at us. There was a little confusion in the 45th caused by some one hollowing fall back. Some started and some stood, but soon all was rallied again. As for my part I determined that I would not give back an inch. . . . But so it was when they got within 20 yards of us we poured a heavy volley into them, and you just ought to have been there to see men & Horses fall. They just fell in every Direction. They came with such force that 3 or 4 horses ran through our lines. From this we got them in full retreat. We runn them through Winchester. They threw away guns, blankets, oilcloths, knapsacks, havresacks, canteens, hats and everything that would impeed their progress. Our boys just loaded themselves with the spoils."[45]

Back at Petersburg, the heart of the Union army was the village of City Point (now Hopewell). Located at the confluence of the Appomattox and James Rivers, it became the central supply depot for all Federal forces engaged in the besiegement. Supply boats crowded the rivers; loaded warehouses covered the adjacent grounds.

Two Confederate secret service agents managed to get a time bomb strategically placed. Just before noon on August 9, "a terrific explosion shook the earth." Grant, sitting in front of his tent, barely escaped injury. Initially, blame was placed on workmen's carelessness. Freeman Colby of the 39th Massachusetts noted: "A barge loaded with ammunition which was being unloaded at the landing, having on board 80 niggers & 3 white men blew up. A man dropped a percussion shell when it exploded, setting the ammunition on fire. Of course all on board perished. The general Post Office & Hamdens Express Office some 20 rods away were blown to fragments, so completely that several thousand dollars of green backs were blown away & lost. The general Hospital covering some 10 acres suffered severely. Our loss in killed & wounded is equal to a general engagement."[46]

Sectors of opposing earthworks were in sight and sound of one another. This produced a series of almost daily incidents. Lieutenant Milton Runkle of the 34th Virginia wrote a cousin: "All is quiet along our lines this morning except the usual picketts fireing. For the las week until a day or so back our picketts & the yanks have been *very* peaceable traiding with each other, until they became too familliar to each other. Genl [Bushrod R.] Johnson came along & saw them laying out togather. He sayd that would not do. He ordered them to fire on the yanks, & since then the pickett fireing has ben very heavy. One at a distance would think that it was a general engagement. You cannot put your head above the works but what their is two or three shots at it."[47]

Portsmouth's Edgar Ashton described a more hated experience. "The last time I was on [picket] I saw several yankee negroes in uniform with their guns and accoutrements walking up and down the bank as big as 'Cuffy.' Neither side are allowed to fire at each other. We do not wait for orders if the negroes are put on the picket line. . . . One of the Villians called to one of our boys, calling 'Jonny, want to know the news?'"[48]

By now, the manpower battle had become hopelessly one-sided. Thanks to the Emancipation Proclamation, thousands of ex-slaves and freedmen were entering Union armies. The Confederacy could not adequately fill the holes made daily in its ranks. On July 23, Sgt. James Anderson of the 57th Virginia noted in his journal: "Got a letter from home. It stated that father had to come into the Service, and all of the men under 50 years of age. I disliked very much that he had to come."[49]

The surrender of Atlanta early in September brought mixed reactions in Lee's army. Major DeShields thought the fall of the much-fought-for city to be "no great loss" to the Confederacy. Still, he added, "it is a big thing for the Yankees to crow over & it is not what we wanted just at this juncture." Private Ashton of the 3rd Virginia observed, "The fall of Atlanta seems to have put a dampers on some of those who were under the impression that we would have an Armistice in a month or two."[50]

Stalemate at Petersburg did not shake the faith either army had in its leader. Robert Stiles of the Richmond Howitzers proclaimed: "Gen. Lee looms up grandly & more grandly still. May God preserve him & grant him the great blessing of living to see a country free, whose children will call him blessed."[51]

Massachusetts soldier Freeman Colby was more

defensive in his loyalty to his commander. "I am sorry people at the north are loosing confidence in Gen. Grant. I know not why they should. . . . It belongs to the private soldiers to find fault if any one. To be sure there [are] some men who never would be satisfied in any position. Such men better not come into the army but stop at home where they can shift as often as they please. I am glad to say there [are] very few such men in the service. . . . There is no other man in the U. S. who has so big a name with us as Grant."[52]

In the Shenandoah Valley, from mid-August to mid-September, the forces of Early and Gen. Philip Sheridan marched and countermarched without becoming engaged. It was a grueling test of mind and body. On September 16, James Cox of the 45th Virginia informed his father: "It is thought this Campaign will wind up this war. I hope it may for I am tiered [of] living sutch a life for there aint any fun in it for I have tried it long enough to know."[53]

Three days later, Sheridan (whose army outnumbered Early by a three-to-one margin) attacked at Winchester. Federals overran Early's left flank and forced the Confederates to fall back 20 miles to a position on dominating ridges called Fisher's Hill. Yet Early lacked a sufficient number of men to hold the four-mile line. On September 22, Sheridan's columns again turned Early's flank, and a rout began. An unknown member of the 13th Virginia described the scene.

"At Fisher's Hill [we] were again flanked on left by cavalry. The whole army broke in great confusion (except the 13th Va Regt which came off in line) and scattered over the whole country, hundreds of the infantry throwing away their guns and going to the mountains. I have never heard any estimate of our loss in prisoners and wagons at either place, but not very great, the greatest loss being the demoralization of the army. I never saw as many men in an army before without [arms]. Neither had I ever seen an army in as bad spirits. They seemed to have lost all confidence in their leader (Early) and in their own ability to resist successfully an attack from the overwhelming force of the enemy."[54]

George Peyton, also in the 13th Virginia, alleged that Early was intoxicated during the battle. "While we were watching the Yankees moving to our rear, Early rode up behind our line, pulled a bottle of whiskey out of his haversack and took a long draft out of it. Perhaps that was the reason he did not know Sheridan had turned his flank. . . . Sheridan completely defeated Early and we left the field a perfect mob."[55]

The lopsided victory resonated through the Union works at Petersburg. Charles Thomas of the 56th Virginia wrote his wife: "We had a tremendous shelling yesterday. The Yankees shot a hundred cannons. They commenced at or near Petersburg, fired all along the lines to James River. I ware on picket and they threw balls and shells all around me but none hurt me. They cut saplins in too in ten feet of my pit. . . . The papers say it was Grants salute for Early's defeat . . . They fired about a our but everything has been quiet ever since."[56]

Sheridan, convinced that the Confederate army was finished, began burning the lower valley in accordance with Grant's orders to reduce the Shenandoah to "a barren waste."[57] In the second week of October, Sheridan submitted a lengthy report of the destruction his men had wrought. The 92 miles between Winchester and Staunton, he boasted, "will have but little in it for man or beast."[58]

Considering the Valley secure, Sheridan began plans to transfer his army back to Grant at Petersburg. A still-defiant Early hastily gathered reinforcements. After an all-night march, Confederates on October 19 made a dawn attack on the Union flank at Cedar Creek. It was a risk-all gamble by Early. Charles Hamilton of the 52nd Virginia gave a telling summary of the action to his parents. "We whip them in the morning and Capterd fifteen Hundard Prisners and 18teen Peaces of Artilury . . . we whip them back five mils Demoralized them vary much but Old Jub was two slow. He let the[m] form again and renforce with towe Devisions, and they Come a gainst ous in the Eavening and they whip ous and demoralized ous vary much and Captered all of the thing which we got from them in the morning. . . . I think we got the worst of it for they out Numbered ous five to one. . . .

"This was a vary hard fite and I hope this will be the last fite that we will hav this winter. I am vary much browken down."[59]

The Shenandoah Valley was now permanently under Union control. No longer could Lee's army look to "The Bread Basket of the Confederacy" for food. As Virginia slowly crumbled, the effect was painfully felt on the home front as well. Mary Smith Morton, who resided in the central Piedmont, wrote her daughter: "I feel the confinement to my work without pleasant episodes of social enjoyment, are making visible inrodes on my constitution. . . . I eat no meat that I may be able to give the servants a little now and then. The butter very small, but so bitter cannot touch it—and I assure you at each meal two corn cakes and weak tea is my sole diet. 'Tis astonishing how little one can do with when necessity becomes your master."[60]

A week later, Mrs. Alexander Graham of Floyd County informed her son, a member of the 54th Virginia: "I would come [to Wytheville] and bring your Clothes but I am a fraid to leve home. The Desertes is so bad here they are agoing in to the peppel houses and taken every thing befor there eyes. They went to Mr. Spirle [Sparrel H.] Griffith hous, taken . . . a hundred Dollars in gold and silver and all of Betty Griffith['s] . . . fine Clothes and fifty bales of Cotton. . . . The Desertes went to Aunt Violets last night. They did not go in to the hous. They taken a turkey. Tily tried to shoute them but he could not get his gun off. They shot at the hous or the dog twice. I just belive they will ruin every body. . . . All of the men in this destrict was notis today to go and hunt for Desertes tomorrow."[61]

Grant's stranglehold on Lee continued for the remainder of the year. There were the occasional skirmishes.

Drayton Pitts, a young recruit in South Carolina's Holcombe Legion, had acquired a girlfriend, Edmonia Mitchell of Sussex County. In his first letter, Pitts described such a clash. "Miss Eddy I expect you hear the fracus that we had that knight. I tell you we had like to have had a right smart row. We was right in frunt of Petersburg that knight and that knight a bout ten oclock the yankeeys pickets charged our pickets and taken 6 of our Legion prisoners. The yankees then held a small portion of our picket line for a bout one hour and thin we charged them and recaptured our picket line and a bout 25 or 30 of the rascals. There was 6 captured, 13 wounded and one kild in the legion."[62]

Quickly the South Carolinians settled into siege warfare. "We have got so that we dont shoot at each other in day time," Pitts wrote. "We just walk a bout through the day and look at each other but then at knight we shoot all the time but that shooting dont amount to much. There is hardly ever a man gets hurt."[63]

The quietness Pitts's unit enjoyed was absent farther along the line. Andrew Friou of the 59th Virginia wrote a long letter to a Brunswick County kinsman. "We are having quite a disagreeable time in the diches. The mud is awfoul and the yankeys wont let us sleep enny a tol in the day time. Tha shell all day and sharp shoot at night. From 4 to 5 are killed and wounded evry day. Lt [William B.] Dickinson was killed last night whiles handing a spade over the Dich to one of the pickets."[64]

In the meantime, brigades were constructing crude huts to combat the coming winter. Jackson Bell of the 5th Virginia gave the details in his area. "The quarters are merely pens made of logs, about 2 ft high, 6 or 7 wide & in length proportioned to the number of men who have to sleep in them. (Some are built for two, others for eight or 10 persons.) Two forks are then drove in the ground, one at each end of the pen, then a pole put across from pole to pole, over which you stretch your oil cloth or tent fly, fastening it to the sides of the pen, and you have a house. It can be put up in an hour & is very comfortable."[65]

Army rations were always scarce. This forced soldiers to turn to anything they deemed digestible. Portsmouth soldier Edgar Ashton told his sister: "I had for my dinner to-day a piece of coon and the first I ever ate and can tell you it was good; before it was cooked some of the men said they would not eat a piece for a $1.00. To-day at dinner we did not have enough for them."[66]

Lack of food took a toll as well on the horses. Joseph Halsey of the 6th Virginia Cavalry wrote his wife in Orange County that scouting "is severe work for cavalry fed on 6 pounds of hay per day & 15 ears of corn per *week*. . . . Our cavalry horses are in bad condition and daily getting worse, and are nearly starved to death. Unless our position is soon changed and supplies are more abundant we shall be utterly unfit for service in two weeks."[67]

Despondency began to settle over Lee's army. Thirty-one-year-old Jackson Bell wrote home: "The men are very tired of the war & long for a cessation of hostilities. I now regret very much that I did not stay at home, not that I am so much dissatisfied here with camp life, but on account of the endless anxiety I feel about you all. I have often thought it w[oul]d have been better if man had been born without what is called natural feeling. If he was dead to all feeling of humanity, especially happy would he be in such times as these."[68]

The 59th Virginia's Jackson Friou felt the same way. "Oh this war wearry me to death. When I think of it I don't see that it is enny nearer to a End now than it was two years ago. I firmly believe old grant will take Petersburg befor he stopes. He has Genl Lees army now so he can besiege it all the winter. I would rather be enny where in the world than under a siege of a contending army. Well there is no us[e] to talk over that."[69]

Lieutenant Garrett of the 3rd Virginia Cavalry was

This pencil sketch may have been the work of a "Capt. Hamil." It shows a small section of a February 1864 encampment at Rappahannock Station (now Remington). The sides of the huts were of logs and mud; the roofs were tents.

willing to talk about it. When his wife suggested a mutual agreement for ending the war, the officer responded: "You spoke of compromise . . . You certainly do not understand the subject or you would see at once there is no room for us to make any such a proposition. Can I compromise with a man who is trying to cut my throat? If I stop my resistance, will he not at once take advantage of it and accomplish his purpose. He can let me alone and thereby we can have peace but I cant—for approvement—cease to defend myself or I am lost. . . . They have determined cooly and calmly to kill every male from infancy to dotage and they argue that it is necessary to do so for their own welfare."[70]

One soldier reached such a pique that he verbally assailed his superiors. "Old Jeff & his satellites are Dictators & excepting Jeff, they have not sense enough to conduct affairs in time of peace, much less in war. We are sold for naught & so they can save their own miserable carcasses. They don't care if the whole Confederacy go to thunder. Even this old Jackass, Jubal Early, has for the last week been trying to make his commands supreme to all civil law. Several men who are in the army have sued out writs & the sheriff came here to serve the writ on the officers in charge & old Early issued an order to arrest the sheriff."[71]

Desertions began to increase; so did military executions.[72] Christmas 1864 was particularly wrenching for Confederates trapped at Petersburg. "I tell you it is the dullest Christmas I ever saw in my life," William Hall of the 51st Virginia wrote his family in Floyd County. "Do wish I could of bin there to of spent Christmas with you all."[73]

Creed Davis of the Richmond Howitzers noted in his diary: "What a pity it is that Santa Claus never visits the Confederate army. We drew this morning a few grains of sugar and coffee, which the Government has kindly condescended, to issue in consideration of Christmas times. Our boys are very despondent to day."[74] Rockbridge County's Jackson Bell summarized his yuletide spirit with few words:

"It was undoubtedly the dullest I ever spent. There was nothing to indicate hollidays or Sabbath either. . . . I spent most of the day around the fire, until in the evening."[75]

One soldier, however, found bliss on the holy day. Drayton Pitts of the Holcombe Legion wrote to his newly acquired sweetheart in nearby Sussex County: "I just received the most butiful pair of gloves that you left. . . . Miss Eddy you said they wer not pretty. You said when you got some nice thread you would make me a fancy pair but oh Miss Eddy I dont know what I can do for you in return for them. Miss Eddy I wouldant take the prettiest fifty dollar bill that I ever saw for them. They are too pretty to ware in camps. I will have to keep them to look at."

Pitts then added: "Miss Eddy you said you had the apple that I gave to you yet I dont know how you keep it so long without it a roting."[76]

As the year drew to a close, Mrs. Mary Morton of Orange County stated to a cousin: "I live among strangers and in a most desolate country; and feel sadly the loss of companionship, of both relations and friends. Evil days have come upon us, but as Christians, must strive to behold 'Gods shining face, behind a frowning providence.'"[77]

1865
"We Had a hard Fite"

"Rations were very scarce," James C. Reed of the Bedford Artillery recalled in the last winter of the war. In the earthworks of Petersburg, most of the Confederate soldiers received "a small quantity of Wausau bacon or pork, with a little corn meal twice a day. The pork caused you to hold your nose to eat it. The little corn pones, or cakes, were not much larger than a silver dollar, and not very much thicker. Two of these twice a day and your belt taken up another hole to make your stomach feel like it was full, we got along finely."[1]

Thoughts of the Southern cause were fading into the distance; human survival was increasingly becoming the issue. Jackson Bell of the 5th Virginia described the greatest need of Confederate soldiers that winter.

"We are not far from starvation. We have been drawing hard bread & pickled beef for a week & only half rations of that & some days none at all. We get about four crackers for a days rations. Our mess (six of us) drew two days rations of beef yesterday, boiled it & eat it all for supper last night & then did not have as much meat as you & I have often ate for one meal. Now if you could see the meat once you would know what it looks like. . . . It smells almost as bad as carrion. We can not live on the rations."[2]

Over in Waynesboro, where the remnant of Gen. Jubal Early's army was encamped, lack of food was painful. Montgomery County native Louis Caldwell informed his sister, "We could do very well here now if they will only give us plenty of rations, which they are shore not to do but perhaps this war may play out some time or another and then we soldiers that have withstood so mutch hardships can rest awhile."[3]

Of the four winters of the Civil War, that of 1864–1865 was the severest. Temperatures plunged; snow fell regularly; roads were always avenues of depthless mud. When the Army of Northern Virginia most needed food, clothing, and shelter, all were in critically short supply.

Floyd County soldier David Hall was among the many who began to despair. "I think the Southern Confererasie will soon go up the spout," he wrote home. "The soldiers are getting very low for clothing and Shoes. I am very near barefooted my self but if they wont cloathe me and shoe me I shant do any duty."[4]

The loneliness was always there. Rockbridge County soldier Jackson Bell confessed to his wife while enduring the freezing elements of trench warfare: "There is but one bright spot in my heart these times & that is a rich oasis formed by a loving & loved female with two bright eyed little cherub boys. Ah! how my heart goes out to them & how the big scalding tear arises when I think of them, & how far I am from them & the slight possibility of ever seeing their dear faces again. But I hope God has better things in store for me than I sometimes imagine."[5]

What might have been a real boost in pride for the entrapped army came on February 6, when Lee received appointment as general-in-chief of all Confederate military forces. The 5th Virginia's Jackson Bell understated feelings in the ranks. Calling Lee now a "Military Dictator," Bell then took the cutting edge from the title. Lee "is a very fine looking man & a very plain looking one. He rides a fine large grey horse & he often leans forward & pats him on the neck. [John B.] Gordon, A. P. Hill or [Henry] Heth either one have more *dash* about them but Lee with his white beard & mild face, commands your respect."[6]

Richmond soldier Howard Walthall was looking heavenward for strength. "We saw the ranks thinning day by day and none knew when his own time would come. We knew we were weak compared to the enemy and nothing but dependence on the great leader above would cause us to prevail."[7]

Quartermaster DeShields saw great promise in Lee's appointment as general-in-chief. "Genl Lee is to command all the armies & confidence is to be restored. This want of confidence—this backing down of the *people*—was the cloud which looked so black, for whilst the military situation was embarrassing it was not hopeless by any means. . . . Genl Lee will hold Richmond . . . God bless him!"[8]

Lee's new assignment might have gained more attention but for a surprise Union offensive. Grant dispatched a large force to cut the Boydton Plank Road, a major Confederate supply artery. Heavy fighting erupted at Hatcher's Run on February 5 and extended over three days. The two sides struggled to a standstill until a snowstorm stopped the engagement. The Union raid produced 2,500 casualties.

Charles Hamilton of the 52nd Virginia sent his mother a personal summary of the action. "We hav had a big fite on the 5. We was ordereded out at day and stay out all day but came in that Night. There was some skirmishen don but know one hert . . . but on Monday we got into it. . . . It [was] the hardest fite that there has been since last fall any whare. There was 86 kild and woned in this Brigade. . . . Col. Huffmin Com[manded] the Brigade. Had his leg taken of below the nee. We lost a Site of offsirs in this Brigad. It seams like the yankees picket for them. Gen John Pegram was kild. Nearly all the Brigade cryed when they herd it. I saw him. He

Buckner McGill Randolph (1842–1903) was captain of the "New Market Volunteers" in the 49th Virginia. He received wounds at both Seven Pines and Cedar Creek. After the war, Randolph was an Episcopal minister until his death in August 1903.

was shot in the Bowels. I was over the Battle field after the fite and there was a site of ded yankees. The men stifen there. But they hav gon back to there winter Qarters and I hope they will stay there."[9]

An even more personal narrative of Hatcher's Run came from the 5th Virginia's Jackson Bell. "No, never, never again do I wish to pass through what I did last Monday evening & night," he wrote his wife. "I did not mind the fighting *very much*, for I felt that I was in [the] hands of one who *could* preserve me. But oh Susie to see the men butchered up, to see them suffering the agonies of death to gratify the ambition of a few men, was heart rending; but worse than this, if possible, was my walk over the battlefield that night. There lay the dead & dying enemy. Each & every one of whom was some ones darling son, brother or husband. And there they lay cold in death, their bodies *stripped* of the few old clothes they had on, & every indignity that could be heaped upon them, was. Nor did the vultures stop at stripping the dead, but there lay the dying, on that bitter cold night, in a state of nudity, not dying fast enough from their wounds, but hastened with freezing. Tuesday morning the ground was covered with sleet & ice, & there was men who still survived their wounds & the cold."[10]

Mixed emotions swirled through Virginia's civilian population that last winter of the struggle. Prince George County's Elizabeth Callender remembered: "It was Feb[ruary] and more apparent every day that our army around Petersbg could not hold the lines much longer. Still there were no complaints and every body hoped for the best."[11] In Richmond, Mary Fontaine expressed her misery by quoting current prices for goods in the capital: shoes, $300 a pair; linen, $111 a yard; butter, $25 a pound; coffee, $150 a pound; tea, $200 a pound; flour, $2,000 per barrel.[12]

Lieutenant Thomas H. B. Randolph of the 2nd Virginia was then a prisoner of war at Johnson's Island, Ohio. His mother in New Market wrote him regularly. When the officer expressed disappointment that he never heard from his father, Dr. Robert Randolph quickly sent a letter. "Lately . . . as troubles have accumulated upon me, I begin to fear, least my Son should think his Father had forgotten him, in his far off Prison House. Oh no my dear Boy, let no such thought enter your mind, but rest assured that I love you, and long to see you the more for every loss that befalls me. The loss of property, I could almost glory in, but to be bereaved of my children, my Boys, is to be bereaved indeed. If then you have felt hurt at my apparent neglect, excuse, forgive, and restore me to the place in your affections which I know that I once held. Two of my cherished hopes are now beneath the sod; let us then, who are left, cling together with a firmer hold, that we may have no sad regrets for short-comings towards each other, when we too may be called upon to part. . . .

"Pray to God my dear Boy, to sustain you in your trials, and in his own good time I doubt not he will grant you liberation."[13]

Among the weeds of war, an occasional seed of romance appeared.

Sampson Meadows and his 36th Virginia were on winter duty in southwest Virginia's "Pewlaskey" County. On March 18, 1865, Meadows wrote Frances Burge, whose Cumberland County husband had been killed in 1863 at Gettysburg:

"My Dear . . . There is talk of disbanding us all and if wee are i wood like verry mutch to pay you a visit. You are a lady that i taken grate fancy to, one that i admire as a lady worthy of eney gentle man though it may be your in ten tion to not had eney communication with eney gentle man. Ef it is not I wont pass eney in sult. i am left just in your condition and i [k]now how it is. i had as fine a lady as ever they sun shind on, but it was god's will to call her away this coming may three yers agon and left mee with three littel children. But thanks bee to god i am able to take care of them. i found out from the peple of appomattox that you was a lady well to doe and hi renown mutch respected by evry body and as fore myself it dont become mee to recommend myself but i will grant you they privledge of riting to giles county to where i was rast and there git my carrecter in full. i will say this mutch that i think I am able to man tane eney lady her days let them bee meney or few. Thats all it becomes mee to say on that subject."[14]

If one lived in the war zone, there was always the danger of Union soldiers plundering and burning. Phillip H. Powers was visiting his family in Scottsville when "Sheridan and his vandals" galloped through town en route to Grant's army. "They behaved dreadfully in the village," Powers charged. Federals seized "about 24 horses, plundered the citizens indiscriminately, robbed the stores of everything in them, and burnt some 27 houses, many of them private residences."[15]

The first three months of the year brought increasing destitution to Lee's troops. That in turn triggered a steady increase in desertions. Drayton Pitts of a South Carolina unit learned that Sherman's Federal army had seized Charleston and Columbia. Worse, Pitts wrote his sweetheart, Yankees were within seven miles of his home. "I have heard it said that the darkest hour was just before day and I think myself that this hour is a geting pretty dark."[16]

Mecklenburg County's George Savage, a captain in the 19th Virginia Heavy Artillery, was equally pessimistic. To an aunt he wrote from Chaffin's Bluff: "The Yankey will begin Very earley in the Spring to make raids. . . . As to our staying where we are I think we will [remain] for some time, but war is Verry uncertain. There is great desertion in our army. Some go to the Yanks every night & *that* will brake up the war sooner than fighting."[17]

Jackson Bell sent home more ominous news from the Petersburg front. "Tell Brother that it's reported here that 172 men left his Div[ision] one night last week & the average number in the whole army is 300 per day." Midway through his letter, however, Bell exulted, "Well Susie we are soon going to whip the yanks & have peace."[18]

Sometimes friendly overtures led to Confederate desertions. On the extreme right of the Southern defenses, the 1st Virginia's Howard Walthall recalled, "was a splendid spring of good water. . . . Often a daring soldier would steal to that hidden spot and meet one from the other side and they would exchange Tobacco for coffee, sugar and newspapers. We were hankering for news and this was our only way to get any, but this familiarity led to bad consequences, because there were many dissatisfied men on our side who preferred prison on the other side to continued hardships on their own, and often they would go away with their newly chosen friends."[19]

Resort to extreme punishment did little or nothing to alleviate the desertion problem. By then, the 5th Virginia's Jackson Bell considered the Civil War as basically a great conspiracy by a group of despots in Richmond. The cynical Bell told his Rockbridge County wife: "There was a man shot to death for desertion. I do not know who he was or where from. He wished to 'live peaceably with all men' & did not wish to violate the 6th commandment [thou shalt not kill], hence he was killed for it. . . . He was tied to *a cross* & shot by twelve men. The effect has been very good & if they shoot a few more the disease will be cured. As an evidence of the good effect, fifteen men have left his regiment this week."[20]

The same soldier announced sneeringly that February 28 was "a day long to be remembered in camp. . . . There was a half pint of whiskey issued to each man [in the regiment] & before night there was hundreds drunk, officers & privates. There was many fights & I never heard more or profaner oaths. Several of them landed in the guard house."[21]

General Grant continued to apply pressure on Lee by extending the Federal lines more and more to the west. This forced Lee to stretch his own thin forces over larger territory. It was like pulling a rubber band to the breaking point. And all the while, Sherman's huge army was driving through North

Carolina and getting closer to Virginia—and Lee's pinned-down force.

"I think we are about gone up the spout. We are now surrounded," Henry W. Baughn of the Confederate Engineers wrote his brother from Petersburg. "I heard just now that the yanks is got old Early prisoner and one half of his army and the other half is a running yet. Thes yanks has come on to Linchburg and got that and I also heard that they have got charlotte and fayetteville N.C. and on there way to Raleigh. . . . I am afraid that we will have to fight the yanks some yet."[22]

Lee decided on a desperate gamble. If he somehow could deliver a crippling blow on Grant, Lee could then leave a holding force at Petersburg and join Confederates trying to stop Sherman's approach. Lee's decision was a forlorn hope, but he had no other option. At dawn on March 25, Confederates stormed Fort Stedman in the center of Grant's defenses. Initially the Confederates were successful; yet like other struggles in the past year, the attack soon lost its momentum. Five hours of fighting produced 4,000 Southern losses, including 2,700 men captured. Survivors fell back to their earthworks.

Comparatively little has been written of the Fort Stedman action. Two Confederates wrote vivid accounts. The 52nd Virginia's Charles Hamilton told his mother in Bath County: "We had a hard fite on the 25th. . . . We charge at 5 oclock in the morning. There was sixty picket sharp shooters chargeed. We toocked the Works with out any one hert but after we got in them they cut us up vary much. There was 3 men got to the Works before I did—I did Not like it but when I got started I wanted to be thrue as quick as possible. My heart Fluterd when I started but when I got in I dident mine it a tall but I tell you It toock men of Courage to charge there Works. . . . God protected me thrue safe. The Yankees had Sheverdefrieze [chevaux-de-frise wooden spikes] out in front of there Works. We had them to cut before we coud git to there Works but we shuceed [succeeded] in d[o]ing all that and then toock the Works . . . but we lost a cite of men and then had to retreat back to our Brest Works and they cut us up vary much. . . . There is 5 of [Company] K left."[23]

Jackson Bell, a late recruit in the Stonewall Brigade, saw Fort Stedman from this perspective: "The fight lasted from ½ past four until 9. I was in sight of most of it & in hearing of all. I never heard such a din & uproar in my life. Mortar shells by the hundred were bursting in the air. Grape, canister & round shot were whizzing thro the air & the musketry was one continued roar. The Yanks soon got in strong reinforcement & our men had to retreat back to our own works. Then it must have been awful, for their infantry poured in volley after volley, while the hill on which was the fort & other batteries looked to me to be a solid sheet of fire. . . . This Co took 25 in the fight & 12 came out. . . . I feel confident that at least one third of this Brigade is killed, wounded or missing & not one thing accomplished."[24]

Now it was Grant's turn. He sent Sheridan with two full army corps and 12,000 cavalry to flank the Confederate right, tear up the last open railroad into Petersburg, and block Lee's escape route to the southwest. Federals caught the enemy napping. At a road junction named Five Forks, Union soldiers overran and routed the Confederate defenders.

Richmond's Howard Walthall was posted that day "near a stream, in a dense woody place where vision didnt extend the length of my regiment. Presently I saw Yankees in hordes coming towards us and realizing certain capture I was quick to obey a command given by a general officer, 'Men, take care of yourselves.' It was difficult to know one direction from another but I decided to take the one leading away from the blue coats and I pushed through the woods, encountering on the way a pack of led horses belonging to dismounted cavalrymen. I climed on the back of one and untieing the reins, got to an open road, filled with fleeing wagons, artillerey and troops."[25]

Born in 1833 in Rockbridge County, Cornelius Jackson Bell studied briefly at Washington College. He joined the 42nd Virginia but left the army in 1862 after hiring a substitute. In October 1864 Bell joined the 5th Virginia. He spent the postwar years at Raphine, where he died in January 1912.

When Grant learned of Sheridan's smashing success, he ordered an assault all along the Petersburg lines at dawn the following day. The roar of battle continued hour after hour; Confederates fought desperately but were slowly driven from one line of trenches to another. By nightfall Lee's battered army of 30,000 troops had crossed the Appomattox River and was retreating westward. Grant, with at least 80,000 soldiers, was in full pursuit.

Meanwhile, the Confederate government was abandoning Richmond. All government property, tobacco, and other valuables of war were ordered set afire. Strong winds late on April 2 turned the flames into an uncontrollable conflagration. Around 1 a.m. on Monday, April 3, young Edward Jones arrived in the city in advance of his Richmond Howitzers. He recalled, "I could notice the confusion which greatly increased as I got well into town, bodies of soldiers marching through the streets, long trains of lumbering wagons, horsemen urging on their steeds carrying messages, citizens burdened with trunks and boxes seeking the [rail] cars, women running hither and thither not knowing what to do or where to go."

Jones made his way through the human mass for an hour or so, then looked back. "Still a dense line pours over the [14th Street] bridge, while already bright fires of boats and warehouses light up the heavens and several deep explosions which shake the city on all its hills . . . Flour, meal, corn scattered everywhere, and valuables of all kinds lay open to the hand of anyone who chooses to take—such are some of the slight consequences of evacuation."[26]

Lee's tattered and hungry army staggered westward, looking for somewhere to stop or something positive to do. Grant's forces dogged the Southerners on three sides. An unknown Billy Yank wrote a week later: "Although I passed through places only a few hours after the reb army did, I never once got a glimps of them. They abandoned their wagons and burned them so as not to be bothered with them and they also cut trees across the road and burned the bridges over the rivers, but for all that the Darkies say that our troops done put up the bridges and catch em before night again and I guess they did for we could not keep up with the troops. The roads were awful muddy and rockey. We marched 10 m[iles] one day and it nearly used us up."[27]

All the while, the South's premier army was disintegrating. "The army went on west in great disorder," the 1st Virginia's Howard Walthall stated, "every man apparently for himself and hundreds falling by the way." Nathaniel Johnston, a member of the "Salem Flying Artillery," recalled that "we pushed our way forward, being harassed all the way by inroads of the enemy's cavalry. During this time many of the Confederates threw away their arms, thus causing the army to become little better than a mob."[28]

Courier David Adkins was at field headquarters on Sunday morning, April 9, when Lee met with his generals. The advisability of making an attack came under discussion. General Fitzhugh Lee, the commander's nephew, exclaimed: "Fight them! Yes, I can break those lines!"[29]

Lee determined to send forward in battle column the troops of Fitzhugh Lee and John B. Gordon. A member of the 8th Virginia Cavalry noted in his diary: "Began the fight early. Several men killed."[30] The advance encountered a thick wall of Union soldiers. Lee was surrounded. There was nowhere for the Confederates to go.

That afternoon, in the front parlor of Wilmer McLean's home in Appomattox, the two commanding generals met. Grant's surrender terms were exceedingly lenient, given the hatred that a civil war usually engenders. Each Confederate soldier was to give his "solemn parole of honor" to cease fighting. In return, each could return home and would "not be disturbed by United States authorities, so long as they observe their parole and the laws in force where they may reside."

Bearing the heavy load of defeat on his weary

shoulders, Lee then had to ride back to his waiting troops. Twenty-year-old Edward Jones of the Richmond Howitzers recorded the unforgettable scene. "In the evening a loud cheer is heard away up on the right. Rushing to the road we see General Lee, hat in hand, riding down toward us. A thunderous cheer seemed to shake the very earth. The old General rode with his head bare and never did he look more noble than then. I tried to join in the cheer but after a faint success my voice stuck in my throat and I could not utter a word. He rode over to his headquarters where many of us followed him. With a trembling voice and a moist eye he made public the terms of our surrender. . . . He excused himself from saying more. The crowd pressed forward to shake hands with him, and now commenced the most affecting scene I ever witnessed. Officers, high in rank, seized his hands with tearful eyes, nor were they more welcome than the weeping privates, each of whom could feel the painful separation. The old General stood with tears in his eyes and welcomed them one by one. It seemed as a grey headed father taking a last farewell of his children. I never witnessed such devotion. . . . I found myself sobbing like a child."[31]

A member of the Salem Flying Artillery remembered the distress of that afternoon: "One of the members of our gun crew . . . who had fulfilled every duty of a soldier faithfully for four years, threw himself down on the ground and wept aloud, bemoaning the fact that four years of such arduous toil had brought such a painful reward."[32]

Pitifully little was left of the once-proud Army of Northern Virginia. Jackson's famous "foot cavalry," the Stonewall Brigade, had contained in all some 6,000 men. At Appomattox it numbered 210 soldiers, none above the rank of captain. Over 1,300 men served in Richmond's 21st Virginia. Two surgeons, a chaplain, and 49 enlisted men were left to surrender.[33]

Charles McVicar of Chew's Battery spoke for all who laid down their arms that Sunday. "It grieved me to part with those boys. Our parting I cannot describe. I had been with most of them for three years. They had stood beside me in so many hard fought battles, had endured hardships, privations, dangers and disasters together and now to part thus, in a manner give up everything we had toiled for."[34]

From Appomattox the Army of Northern Virginia made its final march—into legend.

Head Qrs Army of Tennessee
Near Greensboro N.C. April 27th 1865

General Orders
No. 18

By the terms of a Military Convention made on the 26th inst by Major General W. T. Sherman U.S.A. and General J. E. Johnston C.S.A. the Officers and men of this army are to bind themselves not to take up arms against the United States until properly relieved from that obligation and shall receive guaranties from the United States Officers against molestation by United States authorities so long as they observe that obligation and the laws in force where they reside for these objects duplicate muster rolls will be made immediately and after the distribution of the necessary papers the troops will march under their Officers to their respective States and there be disbanded all retaining personal property the object of this convention is pacification to the extent of the authority of the Commanders who made it

Events in Virginia which broke every hope of success by war imposed on its General the duty of sparing the blood of this gallant army and saving our Country from farther devastation and our people from ruin

Signed J. E. Johnston
General

Official
Signed Archer Anderson
Lt Col & A A G
Official F. B. Ray
A A G

To
Major Manly
Comdg. Artillery

This copy of General Orders No. 18 was the official surrender of the Army of Tennessee to Sherman's forces. Similar in content to the document General Lee signed at Appomattox on April 9, 1865, Johnston's agreement to terms ended the Civil War in the Eastern theater. His farewell to his soldiers was General Orders No. 22, dated May 2, 1865.

Epilogue
"The Fallen Leaves of the Forest"

Virginia had been the principal battleground for four years of the most intense fighting the world had ever witnessed. Destruction blanketed the landscape. John T. Trowbridge, a Northern journalist, visited the state just months after Lee's surrender. Trowbridge saw "no sign of human industry, save here and there a sickly, half-cultivated corn field . . . the country for the most part consisted of fenceless fields abandoned to weeds, stump lots and undergrowth."

The reporter was shocked at the condition of Richmond. "As far as the eye could reach, the business portion of the city bordering on the river lay in ruins. Beds of cinders, cellars half filled with bricks and rubbish, broken and blackened walls, impassable streets deluged with debris, here a granite front still standing and there the iron fragments of crushed machinery . . . Great factories, flour mills, rolling mills, foundries, machine shops, warehouses, banks, railroads, freight and engine houses, two railroad bridges and one other bridge spanning on high piers [over] the broad river had been destroyed."[1]

Wholesale devastation was but part of the war's legacy. The foundation of the South's economic system—slavery—

had been permanently eliminated. Confederate bonds and currency were worthless. Families had been uprooted and scattered. Maintaining law was tenuous and largely lay in the hands of Union soldiers who would keep the Southern states under military occupation for more than a decade.

Even worse was the loss of life. Over 15,000 of Virginia's manhood had died of sickness and battle. A greater number had been shot to pieces. They stumped about on wooden legs, or had empty sleeves, or would suffer the rest of their days from war-induced psychoneurosis, which was then an unknown malady.

In short, Virginia had suffered total defeat. If despondency characterized the present, hopelessness marked the future. William M. West of Eastville informed a friend after a May 1865 visit to the Eastern Shore: "I have been intending to write you since my return from Accomac, and have put it off because I have hardly known how or what to write. The *one* hope of my life that I have for the past four years so fondly cherished being gone—and to all appearances irreparably so. I am wretched, and have little hope of ever living otherwise. Yes I am a miserable man and feel, had I fallen in any of the battles through which I have passed, I should be thankful. A wise and merciful Providence though willed otherwise, and I must think and hope it for the best."[2]

As disfranchised inhabitants of a conquered land, Virginians turned almost instinctively to Robert E. Lee for guidance. The broken and ill general made peace with himself and the new Union. To his soldiers Lee stated, "Go home, all of you boys who fought with me, and help to build up the shattered fortunes of our old state."[3]

Lee himself set an example of reconciliation unmatched by anyone else of his time.

Bitterness of war melted naturally with the passage of time. Portsmouth's Claudius Murdaugh would muse in his ledger: "Alas! The quarter part [of our years] are gone! The silver thread is cut! The golden bowl is broken. A few, a precious few of them yet live—scattered as the fallen leaves of the forest."[4]

David Bailey, who served in the 37th Virginia, stated in recollections done at the request of his family, "The years with all their troubles, pleasures, failures, victories, disappointments & regrets have gone into history and I should approach the coming years with higher resolves & nobler aims for still greater results & achievements." At the close of his memoirs, Bailey said, "After all the old boys have passed over the divide, it would be pleasant to have a reunion."[5]

Veterans' reunions in the postwar years went far in healing the breach. With the passage of time, the stories told by the aging soldiers sometimes grew more humorous and less woeful. One such incident occurred at a 1912 reunion held in Richmond. Sitting under a tree, an old Confederate recalled the Union army using an underground mine to blow a huge hole in the Petersburg line. "When we was blowed up at the Crater, me and my men was th'owed up in the air. As we went up, we met our captain a-comin' down, and as he went by he hollered, 'Rally, boys, when you hit the ground!'"

A well-known scholar wrote of this story: "There was nothing of rancor in their good-natured reminiscences. Gone was the ancient animosity for the 'Yanks.' They talked of the war as though all of the delirium of the sixties had been obliterated by the flood of years."[6]

It was the veterans who took the lead in the long healing process. Just before his death, the 5th Maine's Aaron Daggett declared: "Instead of bitterness, I have love for those noble Confederate veterans. . . . We both fought for what we believed to be right. Both were equally honest."[7]

Johnny Rebs and Billy Yanks could forgive, and none of them ever forgot. In old age they wore a common badge: survivors of a great war that produced a unified nation. The memories they cherished became their connecting links with us who inherited their deeds.

In 1891 Lewis Holt of the 1st Massachusetts Heavy Artillery wrote his sister: "One night last week I laid awake almost all night, my body racked with pain from malarial poison contracted in the miasmatic atmosphere of Virginia, and I went all through the war. I saw every place that I was in during my term of service. I went over every march, and through every battle and skirmish. I was on the picket line, and in the charge. I saw the smoke and heard the din of battle. I saw the foe and heard the rebel yell. I saw every man of Co. H alive and well, and I saw them fall on the field of Spotsilvania, some dead and some wounded. I saw the wounded tenderly taken up and cared for after the battle, and I saw the dead laid in a row side by side, touching elbows as they did in the ranks. I saw the trench dug, and the dead laid in it still touching elbows, their caps over their faces. I heard the short prayer of the Chaplain, a mumbling of a few meaningless words, a disagreeable duty gotten through with as quickly and easily as possible. I saw those who were left of Co. H standing with uncovered drooping heads while tears fell from their eyes as the dirt was, not thrown, but gently pushed in as though taking care not to hurt their poor dead comrades. The strip of hardtack box on which was written the name and killed at Spotsilvania May 19th 1864. I was in the charge again at North Anna river, at Totopotomy and fighting and marching again and it was as real as it was twenty seven years ago.

"Saturday I went out with a full heart to attend memorial services and decorate the graves of the dead soldiers here, and yesterday I sat down and read all about what was done in other places . . ."[8]

Notes

FOREWORD

1. Richard V. Gaines to Jane Watkins Gaines, September 3, 1862, Gaines Family Papers, James I. Robertson, Jr., Legacy Project, Library of Virginia. Unless otherwise cited, all manuscript references are to the Legacy Collection.
2. Claudius W. Murdaugh Ledgers.
3. Walter Lowenfels, *Walt Whitman's Civil War* (New York: Alfred A. Knopf, 1961), 293.

"HOW HARD THE LIFE OF A SOLDIER"

1. Stephen V. Ashe, *When the Yankees Came* (Chapel Hill: University of North Carolina Press, 1995), 3.
2. Betty Gray Fitzhugh Snyder Diary, May 10, 1862, and October 25, 1863.
3. Daniel E. Sutherland, *Seasons of War* (New York: Free Press, 1995), v.
4. Murdaugh Ledgers.
5. Rudolphus W. Cecil to Lizzie, September 12, 1863, Rudolphus Cecil Letters. Cecil died of battle wounds in a June 1864 action.
6. John C. Clarke to Elizabeth Topping, August 16, 1863, John C. Clarke Letters.
7. Thomas W. Fisher to Frances Fisher, October 4, 1862, Fisher Family Letters.
8. John H. Stone to Martha Ann Stone, September 30 and November 23, 1862, Baughn-Stone Letters.
9. Jane W. Gaines to Richard V. Gaines, March 18, 1862, Gaines Papers.
10. Undated poem, Jane Adams Oden to John Beverly Oden, Oden Family Papers. Dr. Oden enjoyed a successful postwar medical career in Martinsburg, West Virginia.

11. James W. Warwick to Miss Maggie, May 13, 1864, James W. Warwick Letter. After the Civil War, Warwick became superintendent of schools for Pocahontas County, West Virginia. "Port-monail" is likely a variant spelling of portmantle, a case for carrying personal effects.

12. Henry C. DeShields to Sarah Wheelright DeShields, June 11, 1863, Henry C. DeShields Papers.

13. James I. Robertson, Jr., *Soldiers Blue and Gray* (Columbia: University of South Carolina Press, 1987), 146–47.

14. H. C. Lawton to cousin, May 12, 1862, Henry C. Lawton Letter.

15. Charles W. Thomas to Mary Pearson Thomas, May 3, 1863, and August 7, 1864, Pearson-Thomas Family Papers.

16. See Benjamin Estep, 33rd Virginia, Death Notice, June 9, 1863; Henry C. Lawton to cousin, May 12, 1862, Henry C. Lawton Letter.

17. Alfred Jay Bollet, *Civil War Medicine: Challenges and Triumphs* (Tucson, AZ: Galen Press, 2002), 366.

18. Milton D. L. Runkle to cousin, September 10, 1861, Runkle Family Papers. Runkle lived in Greene County until his death in 1918.

19. Alexander H. Seiders to wife, December 20, 1862, Alexander Seiders Papers.

20. Charles W. Thomas to Mary P. Thomas, January 9, 1862, Pearson-Thomas Papers.

21. David T. Hall to Sarah Graham, October 28, 1861, Graham-Hall-Shortt Family Papers.

22. Mary Adelaide Burrows Fontaine Diary, February 27, 1864.

23. John Shepherd, Jr., "Religion in the Army of Northern Virginia," *North Carolina Historical Review*, 35:341.

24. John H. Stone to wife, September 30, 1862, Baughn-Stone Letters; Aquilla J. Peyton Diary, April 12, 1863.

25. John 15:13.

26. Thomas W. Fisher to parents, July 28, 1864, Fisher Family Letters.

27. "Civil War Papers of Samuel Edwin Garrett," 18.

28. James Thomas Blair to sister, May 1864, James T. Blair Letter.

1861: "DRIVE BACK THE DASTARD INVADERS"

1. Elizabeth Randolph Meade Callender Recollections.
2. Daniel W. Crofts, *Reluctant Confederates* (Chapel Hill: University of North Carolina Press, 1989), 137.
3. Ibid., 277.
4. Roy P. Basler, ed., *The Collected Works of Abraham Lincoln* (New Brunswick, NJ: Rutgers University Press, 1953–55), 4:331–32.
5. Callender Recollections.
6. Gray Diary, April 15, 1861.
7. *Lynchburg Daily Virginian*, April 16, 1861.
8. "Memoirs of Moses Peter Rucker," 7.
9. Margaret Moss Agee to sister, April 24, 1861, Moss Family Papers.
10. The local unit in question became a company in the 14th Virginia.
11. Henry C. DeShields to Sarah W. DeShields, May 12, 1861,

DeShields Papers.

12. Brother to Austin P. Edwards, May 7, 1861, A. P. Edwards Papers.

13. Andrew J. Nye to son, May 7, 1861, A. J. Nye Letter.

14. Helen Myrick Daughtry to David Myrick, May (?) 1861, Myrick Family Letters.

15. "Civil War Papers of Samuel Edwin Garrett, 3rd Virginia Cavalry, 1861–1865."

16. Fontaine Diary, May 1861; "Civil War Papers of Samuel Edwin Garrett." Nineteen-year-old Howard Walthall joined the "Old Dominion Guard" that became part of the 1st Virginia. "When we got our gray uniforms of short jacket & pants, with canvass leggins & little cap," he declared, "we looked like real soldiers and as we marched through the streets [of Richmond] our breasts puffed with the pride of heroes." Walthall Family Papers, Walthall Recollections. For a bombastic call to arms from Gen. P. G. T. Beauregard to young men in northern Virginia, see U. S. War Dept., comp., *War of the Rebellion: A Compilation of the Official Records of the Union and Confederate Armies* (Washington: Government Printing Office, 1880–1902), Ser. I, 2:907. Cited hereafter as *Official Records*, with all references being to Ser. I.

17. Memoirs of Freeman E. Colby, Colby Family Papers.

18. Walthall Recollections.

19. John C. Adams to family, May 22, 1861, Adams Family Papers.

20. Mary Rebecca Thomas to Charles W. Thomas, July 23, 1861, Pearson-Thomas Papers.

21. John H. Ervine to Ellen W. Ervine, July 27, 1861, Ervine Family Papers.

22. Walthall Recollections. In an excited letter home, James Newlon of the 8th Virginia put battle casualties at six times what they actually were. James Newlon to parents, July 26, 1861, Newlon Family Papers. See also Henry James to Albert, Henry James Letter.

23. Frederick W. Watkins to brother, July 27, 1861, Frederick W. Watkins Papers.

24. *Official Records*, 5:431–32.

25. John Hamilton Ervine to wife, July 27, 1861, Ervine Family Papers.

26. Abraham Vanfleet to parents, September 30, 1861, Abraham Vanfleet Letters.

27. Frederick W. Watkins to mother, October 22, 1861, Frederick W. Watkins Papers.

28. Charles M. Lasley to father, December 25, 1861, Charles M. Lasley Letters.

29. Peter H. Nicholson to C. C. Crouch, August 6, 1861, Peter Nicholson Letter.

30. Lewis G. Holt to sister, August 11, 1861, Caroline Holt Flemings Letters.

31. Joseph T. Embrey to sister, July 14, 1861, Joseph T. Embrey Letter.

32. Milton D. L. Runkle to cousin, August 26, 1861, Runkle Family Papers.

33. James M. Newlon to parents, December 5, 1861, Newlon Papers. In a September 5, 1861, letter to a sister, a Massachusetts soldier at Arlington Heights

twice reported the death of Confederate President Jefferson Davis. Flemings Letters.

34. Arthur C. Cummings to unknown addressee, April 22, 1861, Arthur C. Cummings Letter; Lewis G. Holt to sister, August 29, 1861, Flemings Letters.

35. Charles M. Lasley to "Friends," August 4, 1861, Lasley Letters.

36. Charles W. Thomas to Mary Thomas, August 11, 1861, Pearson-Thomas Papers.

37. Broadside.

38. Ellen W. Ervine to children, October 5, 1861, Ervine Family Papers. The identity of "Black Tongue" is unknown. It is not related to the fourteenth-century bacterial plague "Black Death" that killed some 200 million Europeans.

39. George W. Newlon to Ann Cockrill, December 13, 1861, Newlon Papers.

40. Charles M. Lasley to father, December 25, 1861, Lasley Letters.

41. For a detailed description of McClellan's popularity with his Union soldiers, see Lewis G. Holt to sister, November 24, 1861, Flemings Letters.

42. James M. Newlon to Ann Cockrill, December 18, 1861, Newlon Papers. The best description of the executions of Pvts. Dennis Cochrane and Michael O'Brien is in *Confederate Veteran*, 40:173–74.

43. Joseph William Campbell to Virginia G. McCormick, December 14, 1861, Ott Family Papers.

44. Aquilla J. Peyton Diary, December 31, 1861. A "French furlough," depending on how one viewed it, was an unauthorized leave or temporary desertion.

45. Muscoe Brooks to Elizabeth Coleman, December 23, 1861, Coleman-Griggs Family Papers.

46. Charles W. Thomas to wife, August 19, 1861, Pearson-Thomas Papers.

1862: "CONSCIOUSNESS OF RIGHT AND DUTY"

1. John C. Adams to family, February 4, 1862, Adams Family Papers. Mud was deeper and worse than snow to soldiers. A Union cannoneer in northern Virginia asserted: "Folks up north dont know what mud is. If they want to se mud let them come out to old verginia after a rain." Warren E. Holt to sister, November 3, 1861, Flemings Letters.

2. Thomas W. Newlon to parents, February 15, 1862, Newlon Papers; Adam Kersh to brother, March 1, 1862, Adam Kersh Papers.

3. Mary G. Allen to William Allen, March 22, 1862, Mary G. Allen Letters.

4. David Hicks to wife, May 1, 1862, David F. Hicks Reminiscences; Nathan Cox to Riley C. Cox, April 1, 1862, James Riley Cox Papers.

5. William G. Baughn to sister, February 24, 1862, Baughn-Stone Letters.

6. Milton D. L. Runkle to cousin, February 2, 1862, Runkle Family Papers.

7. Walthall Recollections.

8. Quoted in Ashe, *When the Yankees Came*, 39.
9. Richard V. Gaines to Jane Gaines, January 17, 1862, Gaines Papers.
10. David Hicks to wife, March 13, 1862, Hicks Reminiscences.
11. Wartime memoir, James M. Scates Diaries. The Scates memoir is especially revealing for wartime affairs in the Northern Neck. Major Henry DeShields of Northumberland County was then serving as a brigade quartermaster. Two weeks after the occupation of Fredericksburg, DeShields stated that "a correspondent of the N. York Herald writing from there says that the only smiling faces they met with in town were those of the dogs & contrabands, that all the white adults were stubborn and uncommunicative, quietly smoking their pipes about the corners of the streets & looking thunder at them as they passed along." Henry DeShields to Sarah DeShields, May 11, 1862, DeShields Papers.
12. Gray Diary, April 27, 1862.
13. Frances Fisher to Thomas Winton Fisher, May 30, 1862, Fisher Family Letters.
14. Marshall P. Frantz to Eliza Petty Frantz, April 11, 1862, Frantz-McCauley Family Papers.
15. Walthall Recollections. Of 2,283 Federal losses at Williamsburg, 468 men were killed in action. Confederate losses were 1,560 soldiers. *Official Records*, 11, pt. 2, 450, 566–69, 587–88.
16. Camilla Loyall Diary, May 11, 1862.
17. Marshall Frantz to sister, May 26, 1862, Frantz-McCauley Family Papers.
18. Daniel Brown Diary, May 25, 1862, Daniel Brown Papers.
19. William A. Moss to father, June 2, 1862, Moss Family Papers.
20. George Newlon to parents, June 20, 1862, Newlon Papers.
21. Wyatt W. Akers to Hamilton Willis, undated letter, Willis Family Letters.
22. Robert Gaines Haile Diary, June 2–3, 1862. In Norfolk, Camilla Loyall noted in her journal that Confederates lost 5,000 killed and wounded, plus 15,000 men taken prisoner. Union casualties were less than 4,000 total. However, Loyall added, "the only account [of the battle] we have is what we read in the Northern papers, so we are in a great state of suspense and anxiety." Loyall Diary, June 6, 1862.
23. Sgt. John Wise to uncle, June 21, 1862, John Wise Papers.
24. Robert C. Brown to sister, June 7, 1862, Brown Family Papers; David R. Willis to brother, June 11, 1862, Willis Family Letters. Praise of General Jackson was not unanimous among Confederate officers. A lieutenant from Charlotte County wrote the following month: "I do not like Genl Jackson's way of carr[y]ing on at all. He keeps his troops incessantly in motion, sometimes without apparent cause & always without their having the slightest conception of where they are going or what for. . . . Everything is kept locked up in his own cranium and really sometimes you would think as the Richm[on]d Whig says that he had been bitten by a mad dog—but I will endeavor not to fall out with him as long as success crowns his business." Richard V. Gaines to Jane W. Gaines, July 28, 1862, Gaines Papers.
25. Henry C. DeShields to wife, July 20, 1862, DeShields Papers.
26. Walthall Recollections.

27. Callender Recollections.
28. Frederick W. Watkins to mother, July 6, 1862, Frederick W. Watkins Papers.
29. Lewis Holt to sister, July 16, 1862, Flemings Letters.
30. Henry H. Lockwood to W. P. Nottingham, July 23, 1862, Henry H. Lockwood Letters. This military liberation came two months before Lincoln issued his Emancipation Proclamation. The Delaware-born Lockwood was military commander of the Eastern Shore throughout the 1862–1865 period.
31. Gray Diary, July 9, 1862.
32. Richard V. Gaines to wife, July 23, 1862, Gaines Papers.
33. Warren E. Holt to sister, August 5 and August 25, 1862, Flemings Letters.
34. Charles M. Lasley to father, August 24, 1862, Lasley Letters.
35. Marshall Frantz to sister, September 1862, Frantz-McCauley Family Papers.
36. *Official Records*, 12, Pt. 2, 50–51.
37. Gray Diary, August 8, 1862.
38. Charles M. Lasley to father, August 13, 1862, Lasley Letters.
39. Henry Cranford to wife, September 4, 1862, Henry L. Cranford Papers.
40. Richard V. Gaines to wife, September 3, 1862, Gaines Papers.
41. Ibid., September 8, 1862.
42. John A. Griggs to wife, September 8, 1862, Coleman-Griggs Family Papers. Lieutenant Gaines, in a September 22 letter to his wife, noted that many of the Confederates who fought at Antietam were barefooted. Gaines Papers.
43. James C. Reed, *Some of the Experiences of James C. Reed as a Soldier in the Army of the Confederate States* (n. p., n. d.), 10–11, James C. Reed Papers.
44. Richard V. Gaines to wife, September 18, 1862, Gaines Papers.
45. Ibid., September 28, 1862.
46. Gray Diary, November 9, 1862. A Union soldier observed at the time: "We are encamped about one mile from Warrington village. In the woods their is troops encamped for a mile around us in every direction." A. Knight to mother, November 10, 1862, A. Knight Letter.
47. *Official Records*, 18:382–83, 406.
48. John H. Stone to wife, October 29, 1862, Baughn-Stone Letters.
49. Freeman Colby to parents, October 17 and December 12, 1862, Colby Family Papers.
50. Nancy Fields Franklin to John H. Franklin, September 28, 1862, Franklin Family Letters.
51. Frances Fisher to Thomas Fisher, September 30, 1862, Fisher Family Letters. Private Fisher had already lost two of his three children and a brother to wartime disease. Fisher deserted the army and was with his wife when she died in November. He voluntarily returned to the army. In his next letter home he moaned, "I feel like I would not care how soon the Call would come for me to leave this poor, troublesome world." Fisher to parents, December 11, 1862, ibid. Fisher died in 1921 and is buried in Crockett.
52. Henry Cranford to wife, November 9, 1862, Cranford Papers. For similar feelings, see Charles A. Parker to brother, October 12, 1862, Charles A.

Parker Letter; David Hicks to wife, November 12, 1862, Hicks Reminiscences.

53. David Hicks to wife, November 22, 1862, Hicks Reminiscences; Frederick W. Watkins to Mary Watkins, November 22, 1862, Frederick W. Watkins Papers. Captain Cranford of New York strongly doubted the "wisdom" behind Burnside's strategy. Henry Cranford to wife, November 20, 1862, Cranford Papers.

54. Frederick Watkins to mother, December 22, 1862, Frederick W. Watkins Papers.

55. David Hicks to wife, December 17, 1862, Hicks Reminiscences. See also Moses Crook, 146th New York, to father, December 21, 1862, Crook Family Letters.

56. Aquilla J. Peyton Diary, December 14, 1862.

57. Alexander H. Seiders to Elmira Seiders, January 1, 1863, Seiders Papers.

1863: "OUR LOSS WAS FAR GREATER"

1. Gray Diary, January 1, 1863.
2. Lewis Holt to sister, January 8, 1863, Flemings Letters.
3. David Hicks to wife, January 18, 1863, Hicks Reminiscences.
4. Henry Cranford to wife, January 25, 1863, Cranford Papers.
5. David Hicks to wife, February 14, 1863, Hicks Reminiscences.
6. Matthew B. Wells to father, February 7, 1863, Matthew B. Wells Letter.
7. Henry DeShields to wife, January 25, 1863, DeShields Papers.
8. Henry DeShields to wife, January 29, 1863, ibid.
9. Henry Douglas Puckett, "Just One of the Unsung Heroes," 20.
10. Burwell Hall to cousins, January 15, 1863, Graham-Hall-Shortt Family Papers.
11. David Hall to cousins, March 13, 1863, ibid.
12. Henry DeShields to wife, April 26, 1863, DeShields Papers.
13. Claudius Murdaugh, "The Battle of Chancellorsville," Murdaugh Ledgers; Frederick W. Watkins to mother, May 9, 1863, Frederick W. Watkins Papers.
14. Murdaugh, "Chancellorsville," Murdaugh Ledgers. See also Eva Robinson Letter.
15. Murdaugh, "Chancellorsville," Murdaugh Ledgers.
16. W. M. West to Mary Fitzhugh, June 6, 1863, Fitzhugh Family Papers.
17. James I. Robertson, Jr., ed., "'The Boy Artillerist': Letters of Colonel William Pegram, C.S.A.," *Virginia Magazine of History and Biography*, 98 (1990): 238; Gray Diary, May 14, 1863.
18. Ausbert G. L. Van Lear to wife, May 1863, Ausbert G. L. Van Lear Collection.
19. Henry Cranford to wife, May 10, 1863, Cranford Papers.
20. Henry DeShields to Sarah DeShields, May 22, 1863, DeShields Papers.
21. See James E. Burge, 18th Virginia, to Frances Burge, June 21, 1863,

James E. Burge Papers; M. Brock, Federal soldier, to brother, June 22, 1863, M. Brock Letter.

22. "Civil War Diary of Charles William McVicar," 9–10.

23. John Minix to wife, June 16, 1863, Minix-Tynes Family Papers.

24. Lewis Holt to sister, June 25, 1863, Flemings Letters.

25. Walthall Recollections.

26. John Winn Moseley to mother, July 4, 1863, Coleman-Moseley Family Papers.

27. Henry DeShields to mother, August 6, 1863, DeShields Papers.

28. "Civil War Diary of Charles William McVicar," 22–23.

29. John C. Adams to family, July 19, 1863, Adams Family Papers. See also Gray Diary, July 11, 1863.

30. Nannie Simpson Bowie to Mary J. Bowie, July 7, 1863, Bowie-Brown Family Letters.

31. Christopher Columbus Crouch to F. D. McRae, September 9, 1863, C. C. Crouch Letter.

32. Andrew J. Graham to cousins, August 8, 1863, Graham-Hall-Shortt Family Papers.

33. John C. Clarke to Elizabeth Topping, September 19, 1863, John C. Clarke Letters.

34. John A. Cummins to brother, August 15, 1863, John A. Cummins Papers.

35. "Civil War Diary of Charles William McVicar," 19–20.

36. John C. Clarke to Elizabeth Topping, October 21, 1863, John C. Clarke Letters.

37. Henry DeShields to Sarah DeShields, October 19, 1863, DeShields Papers.

38. Fontaine Diary, November 10, 1863.

39. John C. Clarke to Elizabeth Topping, December 6, 1863, John C. Clarke Letters.

40. Gray Diary, December 25, 1863.

41. Henry DeShields to Sarah DeShields, December 29, 1863, DeShields Papers.

1864: "THIS CRUEL WAR"

1. George Washington McSwain to Hanna McSwain, January 3, 1864, G. W. McSwane Letter. (The original document is a newspaper clipping in which McSwain's name is misspelled.) Three other members of Lee's army were shot for desertion the same month. *Richmond Daily Dispatch*, January 15, 1864; *Lynchburg Daily Virginian*, January 18, 1864. The following month, writing from Washington County, Lt. James Cox of the 45th Virginia stated: "There is a man to be shot on the 26th of this inst in our Regt. I don't care to see the sight my self." James R. Cox to brother, February 20, 1864, James Riley Cox Papers.

2. Gray Diary, January 21, 1864.

3. Morris Whetzel to cousin, January 20, 1864, Morris Whetzel Letters. The Winchester native survived the war.

4. Thomas B. Jones to brother-in-law, January 21, 1864, Pearson-

Thomas Papers. Jones was killed in action near Petersburg on July 12, 1864.

5. Edgar E. Ashton to "Aunt Betsy," February 27, 1864, Edgar Ashton Letters.

6. Eli Coffelt to wife, February 22, 1864, Eli Coffelt Letter. A first sergeant at his surrender, Coffelt had a long postwar career in Shenandoah County.

7. Daniel D. Cox to parents, April 7, 1864, Daniel D. Cox Papers. A month later, Cox was captured at Spotsylvania. He died March 7, 1865, of diarrhea at Elmira Prison, New York.

8. Henry DeShields to wife, April 7, 1864, DeShields Papers.

9. Nathaniel Moon Cleveland to Thomas Cleveland, April 1, 1864, Nathaniel M. Cleveland Letter.

10. John Clarke to Elizabeth Topping, January 5, 1864, John C. Clarke Letters.

11. David T. Hall to cousins, March 29, 1864, Graham-Hall-Shortt Family Papers.

12. Edgar Ashton to "Aunt Betsy," April 20, 1864, Edgar Ashton Letters.

13. Unidentified Letter, May 4, 1864.

14. "Franklin Gardner Walter: His Civil War Diary and Letters."

15. Ann R. Hudson to Jane Moss, July 10, 1864, Moss Family Papers.

16. George T. Stevens, *Three Years in the Sixth Corps* (New York: D. Van Nostrand, 1870), 340.

17. "Civil War Diary of Charles William McVicar," 32. David T. Hall of the 51st Virginia added: "We run the yanks a bout 5 mils and tha cross the river this side of mount Jackson and burnt the brig so we had to stop but the[y] cep retreating. . . . I went out on the field next day and . . . the boys got a hep of one thing a nother." David T. Hall to cousins, May 19, 1864, Graham-Hall-Shortt Family Papers.

18. Statement dated May 23, 1864, Zeiler Family Papers.

19. Walthall Recollections.

20. Freeman Colby to parents, May 14, 1864, Colby Family Papers; "Reminiscences of George Q. Peyton," 20, 25.

21. "Franklin Gardner Walter: His Civil War Diary and Letters," 28; David T. Hall to family, May 26, 1864, Graham-Hall-Shortt Family Papers.

22. Helen Green Stewart to Robert Green, May 26, 1864, Helen G. Stewart Letter.

23. Peyton, "Reminiscences," 26. For a vividly revealing description of the Cold Harbor battleground after the struggle, see "Civil War Diary of Charles William McVicar," 49–50.

24. "Civil War Diary of Charles William McVicar," 50. See also Walthall Recollections.

25. Joseph J. Halsey to Mildred Halsey, May 31, 1864, Halsey Family Papers.

26. Henry Cranford to wife, June 10, 1864, Cranford Papers.

27. Peyton, "Reminiscences," 28.

28. Louise Humphreys Carter Reminiscences.

29. Joseph J. Halsey to Mildred Halsey, June 22, 1864, Halsey Family Papers.

30. Freeman Colby to parents, June 24, 1864, Colby Family Papers.
31. Charles Thomas to Mary Thomas, July 1, 1864, Pearson-Thomas Papers.
32. "Civil War Diary of Charles William McVicar," 45.
33. Freeman Colby to parents, June 24, 1864, Colby Family Papers.
34. Quoted in J. Tracy Power, *Lee's Miserables: Life in the Army of Northern Virginia from the Wilderness to Appomattox* (Chapel Hill: University of North Carolina Press, 1998), 112.
35. "James Anderson's Book," 6.
36. Ibid., 10.
37. Charles W. Thomas to wife, July 24, 1864, Pearson-Thomas Papers.
38. Henry DeShields to wife, July 4, 1864, DeShields Papers.
39. Henry DeShields to wife, July 6, 1864, ibid.
40. Peyton, "Reminiscences," 32–33. If Peyton was referring to Captain James Jones White, a Washington College professor who commanded the "Liberty Hall Volunteers" of the 4th Virginia, he was in error. White survived the war.
41. Ibid., 36.
42. David F. Bailey Reminiscences.
43. Thomas W. Fisher to parents, July 28, 1864, Fisher Family Letters. In May, Gen. George Crook had led a raid that severed the Virginia & Tennessee Railroad at Dublin. A month later, Gen. David Hunter started through the Valley on a probe that ended disastrously at Lynchburg. For another account of Early's threat on Washington, see James R. Cox to father, July 10, 1864, James Riley Cox Papers.
44. Henry Cranford to wife, July 8, 1864, Cranford Papers.
45. Thomas W. Fisher to parents, July 28, 1864, Fisher Family Letters. For a briefer account of Second Kernstown, see James Riley Cox to sister, August 1864, James Riley Cox Papers.
46. Freeman Colby to parents, August 10, 1864, Colby Family Papers. Casualties from the City Point explosion were 58 killed and 126 wounded. *Official Records*, 42, Pt. 1, 955.
47. Milton D. L. Runkle to cousin, August 8, 1864, Runkle Family Papers.
48. Edgar Ashton to aunt, September 9, 1864, Edgar Ashton Letters.
49. "James B. Anderson's Book," July 9, 1864.
50. Henry DeShields to wife, September 15, 1864, DeShields Papers; Edgar Ashton to aunt, September 9, 1864, Edgar Ashton Letters.
51. Quoted in Power, *Lee's Miserables*, 203.
52. Freeman Colby to parents, September 2, 1864, Colby Family Papers.
53. James R. Cox to father, September 16, 1864, James Riley Cox Papers.
54. Unidentified Confederate Soldier Letter, October 27, 1864.
55. Peyton, "Reminiscences," 56.
56. Charles W. Thomas to Mary Thomas, September 24, 1864, Pearson-Thomas Papers.
57. *Official Records*, 43, Pt. 1, 917. Valley residents found within five miles of a railroad could be imprisoned—and might be shot. Ibid., Pt. 2, 348.

58. *Official Records*, 43, Pt. 2, 308.

59. Charles A. Hamilton to parents, October 22, 1864, Charles A. Hamilton Letters. For a detailed account of the fighting at Cedar Creek, see Frank ____ (who served in the Charlottesville Artillery) to brother Catlett, October 27, 1864, Unidentified Confederate Soldier Letter.

60. Mary Smith Morton to Mildred Morton Halsey, October 9, 1864, Halsey Family Papers.

61. Lucinda Graham to son, October 16, 1864, Graham-Hall-Shortt Family Papers.

62. Drayton Pitts to Edmonia Mitchell, October 30, 1864, Drayton S. Pitts Letters. An official report of the action is in *Official Records*, 42, Pt. 2, 933.

63. Drayton Pitts to Edmonia Mitchell, November 28, 1864, Drayton S. Pitts Letters.

64. Andrew J. Friou to sister, November 27, 1864, Binford-Friou-Johnson Family Papers.

65. C. Jackson Bell to wife, November 18, 1864, Cornelius Jackson Bell Papers.

66. Edgar Ashton to sister, October 31, 1861, Edgar Ashton Letters.

67. Joseph J. Halsey to Mildred Halsey, December 24, 1864, Halsey Family Papers.

68. C. Jackson Bell to wife, November 18, 1864, Cornelius Jackson Bell Papers.

69. Andrew J. Friou to sister, November 27, 1864, Binford-Friou-Johnson Family Papers.

70. "Civil War Papers of Samuel Edwin Garrett," 20.

71. C. Jackson Bell to wife, December 2, 1864, Cornelius Jackson Bell Papers.

72. See David J. L. Snidow to sister, December 23, 1864, Guthrie-Snidow Family Papers.

73. William L. Hall to family, December 26, 1864, Graham-Hall-Shortt Family Papers.

74. Quoted in Power, *Lee's Miserables*, 230.

75. C. Jackson Bell to Susan Bell, December 31, 1864, Cornelius Jackson Bell Papers.

76. Drayton Pitts to Edmonia Mitchell, December 24, 1864, Drayton S. Pitts Letters.

77. Mary Smith Morton to Daniella Morton Grinnan, December 30, 1864, Halsey Family Papers.

1865: "we had a hard fite"

1. Reed, *Experiences*, 26–27, James C. Reed Papers. The 55th Virginia's John Clarke lacked a sense of army humor. To his future wife in mid-January 1865 Clarke declared: "Times are very dull with the soldiers now. They are in very low spirits about the war." John C. Clarke Letters.

2. C. Jackson Bell to Susan Bell, January 1, 1865, Cornelius Jackson Bell Papers.

3. Louis B. Caldwell to Agnes Caldwell, January 18, 1865, Louis

Caldwell Letter.

    4. David T. Hall to family, January or February 1865, Graham-Hall-Shortt Family Papers. For similar sentiments, see John C. Clarke to Elizabeth Topping, January 15, 1865, John C. Clarke Letters; J. J. Halsey to Mildred Halsey, January 17, 1865, Halsey Family Papers.

    5. C. Jackson Bell to Susan Bell, January 14, 1865, Cornelius Jackson Bell Papers. Bell lived a happy and prosperous life until his 1912 death.

    6. C. Jackson Bell to Susan Bell, February 15, 1865, ibid.

    7. Walthall Recollections.

    8. Henry DeShields to wife, January 25, 1865, DeShields Papers.

    9. Charles A. Hamilton to mother, February 10, 1865, Charles A. Hamilton Letters. Colonel John Stringer Hoffman lost a foot at Hatcher's Run but after the war became a judge in Clarksburg, West Virginia. General John Pegram's funeral was held in the same Richmond church where he was married a month earlier.

    10. C. Jackson Bell to Susan Bell, February 11, 1865, Cornelius Jackson Bell Papers.

    11. Callender Recollections.

    12. Fontaine Diary, March 1865.

    13. Robert Randolph to Thomas H. B. Randolph, February 1865, Robert C. Randolph Letter. The son was on Gen. William N. Pendleton's staff when captured. He died in 1900 in Milford.

    14. Sampson G. Meadows to Frances Burge, March 18, 1865, James E. Burge Papers. Meadows died in 1879 in Mercer County, West Virginia.

    15. Phillip H. Powers to "Mrs. Ware," March 27, 1865, Phillip Powers Letter. For Gen. Thomas C. Devin's report of some of the damage done at Scottsville, see *Official Records*, 46, Pt. 1, 490.

    16. Drayton Pitts to Edmonia Mitchell, February 22, 1865, Drayton S. Pitts Letters. Pitts was killed in a March 31 action at White Oak Road.

    17. George S. Savage to sister, January 22, 1865, G. S. Savage Letter.

    18. C. Jackson Bell to Susan Bell, January 15, 1865, Cornelius Jackson Bell Papers.

    19. Walthall Recollections. See also C. Jackson Bell to Susan Bell, March 15, 1865, Cornelius Jackson Bell Papers.

    20. C. Jackson Bell to Susan Bell, February 11, 1865, Cornelius Jackson Bell Papers.

    21. C. Jackson Bell to Susan Bell, March 1, 1865, ibid.

    22. Henry W. Baughn to brother, March 5, 1865, Baughn-Stone Letters.

    23. Charles A. Hamilton to mother, March 29, 1865, Charles A. Hamilton Letters.

    24. C. Jackson Bell to Susan Bell, March 26, 1865, Cornelius Jackson Bell Papers. See also Andrew Friou, 59th Virginia, to sister, March 26, 1865, Binford-Friou-Johnson Family Papers.

    25. Walthall Recollections.

    26. "Diary of Edward Valentine Jones," April 3, 1865.

    27. Arthur to mother, April 14, 1865, Unidentified Union Soldier Letter. For destruction by Union cavalry during this campaign, see James Galt to

Abraham Shepherd, March 29, 1865, James Galt Letter.

    28. Walthall Recollections; "Civil War Reminiscences of Nathaniel Burwell Johnston," April 8, 1865.

    29. Chesterfield and Colonial Heights *News-Journal*, May 5, 1960, in D. D. Adkins Reminiscences.

    30. John A. Davidson Diary, April 9, 1865.

    31. "Diary of Edward Valentine Jones," April 9, 1865.

    32. "Civil War Reminiscences of Nathaniel Burwell Johnston," 10.

    33. 21st Virginia Infantry Regiment Roster.

    34. "Civil War Diary of Charles William McVicar," 72.

EPILOGUE: "THE FALLEN LEAVES OF THE FOREST"

    1. John T. Trowbridge, *The Desolate South, 1865–1866* (Boston: Little, Brown and Company, 1956), 50, 52, 83–85.

    2. W. M. West to Mary Macon Fitzhugh, May 19, 1865, Fitzhugh Family Papers.

    3. Douglas Southall Freeman, *R. E. Lee: A Biography* (New York: Charles Scribner's Sons, 1934–35), 4:191–92.

    4. Murdaugh Ledgers.

    5. David F. Bailey Reminiscences.

    6. Virginius Dabney, *Virginius Dabney's Virginia* (Chapel Hill: University of North Carolina Press, 1986), 166.

    7. Aaron S. Daggett to "Miss Rouse," July 1, 1936, Aaron S. Daggett Letter.

    8. Lewis Holt to sister, June 11, 1891, Flemings Letters.

ILLUSTRATION CREDITS

Photos and other images came from the James I. Robertson Jr. Civil War Sesquicentennial Legacy Collection of the Library of Virginia, accessible online at www.virginiamemory.com/collections/cw150.

Page 17, Unidentified woman, ca. 1860–1870. Contributed by Robert B. Thomas III.

Page 28, Joseph Lee Minghini photograph, 1863. Copy of original contributed by Jim Garrett.

Page 35, John Floyd Walker, ca. 1861–1865. Contributed by J. Tracy Walker III.

Page 48, Peter Lee Huddleston, in Peter L. Huddleston Papers, 1862–1953. Contributed by Sheila E. Baker.

Page 74, Child photograph, undated. Contributed by Douglas L. Stegall and Stuart L. Schricker.

Page 81, Howard and Robert Walthall, in Walthall Family Papers, 1866–1916. Contributed by Grace Turner Karish.

Page 89, George Baxter Hannah and Albert Gallatin Jenkins, in George B. Hannah Photographs, undated. Contributed by William C. Flournoy.

Page 98, Drawing of Rappahannock Station (Va.), February 8, 1864. Contributed by Robert W. Rich.

Page 104, B. M. Randolph photograph, ca. 1861–1865. Contributed by J. Tracy Walker III.

Page 111, Cornelius Jackson Bell photograph, in Cornelius Jackson Bell Papers, ca. 1864–1875. Contributed by Anne Bell Scott.

Page 116, General Orders No. 18, in Price Family Papers, 1858–1865. Contributed by Carol Williams.

Index

All place names are in Virginia unless otherwise noted.

Accomac County, 118
Adams, John C., 39
Adkins, David D., 113
African-Americans: as slaves, 14–15, 26, 34, 47, 68; as soldiers, 86–87, 92
Agee, Margaret Moss, 25
Akers, Wyatt W., 45
Alabama Infantry Regiment: 6th, 45
Albright, James C., 86
Alexandria, 31
Allen, Mary Garrett, 39
Allen, William, 39–40
Amherst County, 39, 78
Anderson, James B., 86, 92
Antietam Creek, Md., 51–52, 54
Appomattox, 113–16
Arlington, 32, 123n33
Ashby, Turner, 43
Ashton, Edgar, 73, 76, 92, 97
Atlanta, Ga., 92
atrocities, 31–32, 50, 53, 73, 82, 94, 107, 130n57, 132–33n
Augusta County, 37, 61
Averell, William Woods, 90

Bailey, David Flournoy, 88, 119
Bath County, 109
battlefields, 8, 30–31, 45, 67, 77–78, 83
Baughn, Henry Whittler, 109
Baughn, William G., 40
Beauregard, Pierre Gustave Toutant, 42, 79, 123n16
Bedford County, 19, 25, 48, 53
Bell, Cornelius Jackson, 96, 97, 99–102, 107, 108, 110, 111, 132n5
Belle Isle Prison, 68
Belle Plain, 58
Blair, James Thomas, 22
Botetourt County, 35
Bowie, Nannie Simpson, 65
Brandy Station, 62, 65
Breckinridge, John Cabell, 78, 90
Bristoe Station, 67
Bristol, 88
Brockenbrough, John Mercer, 87
Brooks, Muscoe, 38
Brown, Daniel, 44
Brown, John, 23, 24
Brown, Robert C., 46
Brunswick County, 96
Burge, Frances, 106
Burnside, Ambrose Everett, 54–55, 57–58, 76, 127n53
Burrows, John Lansing, 68

Caldwell, Louis, 102
Callender, Elizabeth Randolph Meade, 24, 47, 105
Cameron, John G., 16
Cameron, Simon, 30
Camp Alleghany, W.Va., 37–38
Camp Lee, 27, 29
Campbell, Joseph William, 37

Campbell, Tarlton, 36
Caroline County, 58
Carter, Louise Humphreys, 84
Cedar Creek, 94–95, 104, 131n59
Cedar Mountain, 50
Centreville, 39
Chaffin's Bluff, 107
Chancellorsville, 59–61, 63
chaplains, 32, 49, 114, 120
Charleston, S.C., 24, 107
Charleston, W.Va., 89
Charlotte County, 8, 16, 41, 51
Charlottesville, 46
Chesterfield County, 37
Christmas, 36, 38, 56, 68, 99–100
City Point, 91, 130n46
Clarke, John Cornelius, 16, 66, 67, 68, 76, 131n1
Clarksburg, W.Va., 132n9
Cleveland, Nathaniel Moon, 75–76
Coffelt, Eli, 73
Colby, Freeman Eri, 27, 53, 80, 85, 91, 92–93
Cold Harbor, 82–83, 129n23
conscription, 92
Cox, Daniel DeJarnett, 75
Cox, James Riley, 93
Cox, Nathan, 40
Cranford, Henry Lloyd, 50, 54, 83, 88
Crook, George, 130n43
Cross Keys, 46
Crouch, Christopher Columbus, 66
Culpeper County, 50, 66, 67
Cumberland County, 25, 27, 45, 106
Cummings, Arthur Campbell, 34

Daggett, Aaron Simon, 119
Dandridge, William, 68
Daughtry, Helen Myrick, 27
Davis, Creed Thomas, 99
Davis, Jefferson, 57, 68, 99, 124n33

death, 18, 64, 120
desertion, 66, 71, 95, 99, 107–8, 126n51, 128n1
DeShields, Henry Clay, 19, 26, 58, 61–62, 64, 67, 68–69, 86, 92, 103, 125n11
Devin, Thomas Casimer, 132n15
diarrhea, 19–20, 42, 129n7
Dickinson, William B., 96
Dinwiddie County, 26
Dix, John Adams, 31, 53
doctors. *See* surgeons
Douglass, Frederick, 14–15
Dranesville, 65
Drewry's Bluff, 21, 79–80
drill, 27, 29
Dublin, 88
Dumfries, 39

Early, Jubal Anderson, 87–88, 93–94, 99, 102, 109
Eastern Shore, 31, 47, 118
Eastville, 118
Edwards, Austin P., 26
Elmira Prison, N.Y., 129
Emancipation Proclamation, 92, 126n30
Embrey, Joseph T., 33
Ervine, Ellen Weir, 36
Ervine, John Hamilton, 30, 31
Essex County, 38, 45, 51
Ewell, Richard Stoddert, 63
executions, 37, 71–72, 99, 108, 124n42, 128n1

family ties, 29–30, 73–75, 102, 106
Farnham Church, 87
Fauquier County, 9, 15, 25, 50, 68
Fisher, Frances, 42
Fisher, Thomas Winton, 16, 21–22, 54, 88, 90, 126n51
Fisher's Hill, 22, 93–94

Five Forks, 110, 112
Floyd County, 21, 59, 76, 95, 99, 102
Fontaine, Mary Adelaide Burrows, 68, 105
food, 29, 36, 42, 58, 65, 80, 82, 95, 97, 101–2
Fort Stedman, 109–10
Fort Sumter, S.C., 24
Franklin, Benjamin, 14
Franklin, Nancy Fields, 53–54
Frantz, Marshall Petty, 44, 49
fraternization, 59, 91, 96, 107
Frederick, Md., 51, 88
Fredericksburg, 38, 41–42, 55, 63, 78, 125n11
"French furloughs," 38, 124n44
Friou, Andrew Jackson, 96, 97

Gaines, Jane Watkins, 16
Gaines, Richard Venable, 8, 41, 49, 51–52
Garrett, Samuel Edwin, 22, 27, 97, 99
Gettysburg, Pa., 63–66, 81, 106
Giles County, 26, 35
Glendale, 46
Goggin, William Leftwich, 25
Gordon, John Brown, 90, 103, 113
Gordonsville, 49
Graham, Alexandria Lucinda, 95
Graham, Andrew Jackson, 66
Grant, Ulysses Simpson, 76, 80, 83, 84, 85–86, 88, 91, 94, 108–10, 112, 113; described, 77, 83; praised, 92–93
Gray, Betty. *See* Snyder, Betty Gray Fitzhugh
Greene County, 33, 40
Griffith, Sparrel H., 95
Griggs, John A., 51

Haile, Robert Gaines, 45
Hall, Burwell R., 59

Hall, David T., 59, 76, 80, 102
Hall, William L., 99
Halsey, Joseph Jackson, 83, 97
Hamilton, Alfred J., 36
Hamilton, Charles Alexander, 94–95, 103, 105, 109–10
Hannah, George Baxter, 89
Harpers Ferry, W.Va., 23, 29, 63
Harrell, James, 16
Hatcher's Run, 103, 105, 132n9
Heathsville, 26, 59
Henry County, 16, 21, 40, 53
Heth, Henry, 67, 103
Hicks, David F., 40, 41, 55, 57–58
Hill, Ambrose Powell, 67, 103
Hoffman, John Stringer, 103, 132n9
Holt, Lewis Garrison, 34, 47, 57, 120
Holt, Warren Eugene, 49
homesickness, 15–16, 40, 59, 73, 75
Hooker, Joseph, 58, 59–61, 76
Hopewell. *See* City Point
horses, 46, 55, 60, 85, 90, 97
House, Alexander Wesley, 34, 36
Howell, William James, 9, 11
Huddleston, Peter Lee, 48
Hudson, Ann R., 78
Hudson, Shelton, 78
Humphreys, George S., 84
Hunter, David, 87, 130n43

insects, 36, 49, 52, 53, 85, 86

Jackson, Cheryl, 11
Jackson, Thomas Jonathan, 43–44, 47, 50, 51; criticized, 49, 125n24; grave of, 87; praised, 30, 60–61
jaundice, 39, 53
Jenkins, Albert Gallatin, 89
Johnson, Bushrod Rust, 91
Johnson's Island Prison, Ohio, 105
Johnston, Joseph Eggleston, 45, 49, 116

Johnston, Nathaniel Burwell, 113
Jones, Edward Valentine, 112, 114
Jones, Thomas B., 73

Kernstown, 43, 90–91, 130n45
Kerr, George, 47
Kersh, Adam Wise, 39

Lasley, Charles M., 36, 49
Lawton, Henry C., 19
Lee, Fitzhugh, 113
Lee, Robert Edward, 45, 47, 50–51, 53, 55, 62–63, 65, 67, 68, 76, 83, 85, 87, 88, 108–9, 112–14; described, 102–3; praised, 60, 80, 92, 103, 114, 118
Leesburg, 34, 51
letter writing, 16, 18, 66
Lexington, 87
lice. *See* insects
Lincoln, Abraham, 23, 24, 26, 29, 31, 75, 77, 84
Lockwood, Henry Hayes, 47, 126n30
Loudoun County, 33
Loyall, Camilla, 44, 125n22
Lynchburg, 81, 87, 88, 109, 130n43

mail. *See* letter writing
Maine Infantry Regiment: 5th, 119
Malvern Hill, 46–47
Manassas, 20, 36, 40; 1861 battle of, 30, 123n22; 1862 battle of, 8, 38, 50–51
marches, 43, 46, 51, 67, 112–13
Martinsburg, W.Va., 28, 121n10
Massachusetts Heavy Artillery Regiment: 1st, 33, 120
Massachusetts Infantry Regiments: 2nd, 44; 13th, 40, 57–58; 39th, 27, 53, 85, 91
McClellan, George Brinton, 36, 43–44, 46, 47, 54, 76, 84, 124n41

McDowell, Irvin, 50, 76
McLean, Wilmer, 113
McSwain, George Washington, 71–72
McVicar, Charles William, 62, 65, 85, 114–15
Meade, George Gordon, 63, 67
Meadows, Sampson G., 106–7
measles, 20–21, 29, 34
Mecklenburg County, 20, 26, 29, 73, 86, 107
Mercer County, W.Va., 132n14
Middleburg, 41
Middlesex County, 16, 66, 76
Milford, 132n13
Milroy, Robert Hutson, 63
Minghini, Joseph Lee, 28
Minix, John, 63
Mitchell, Edmonia, 96
Montgomery County, 45, 102
Morton, Mary Smith, 95, 100
Moseley, John Winn, 64
Moss, William Ajax, 45
Mount Jackson, 129n17
"Mud March," 58
Murdaugh, Claudius Walke, 9, 15, 60, 118–19
Myrick, David, 27
Myrick, Helen, 27

Narrows, 59
Nelson County, 78
New Jersey Infantry Regiment: 1st, 31
New Market, 78–79, 104
New York Infantry Regiments: 14th, 50; 76th, 78
New York Light Artillery Regiment: 4th, 32, 55
Newlon, George W., 36, 45
Newlon, James M., 33–34, 37, 123n22
Newlon, Thomas, 39
Newman, Conway, 87
newspapers, 34, 125n11, 125n22,

125n24
Norfolk, 44, 53, 125n22
North Anna River, 120
North Carolina Infantry Regiments: 21st, 49; 34th, 71; 45th, 40
Northern Neck, 26, 58, 86, 125n11
Northumberland County, 61, 86, 125n11
Nye, Andrew Jackson, 26

Oden, Jane Adams, 16, 18
Oden, John Beverly, 16, 18
Orange County, 16, 66, 71, 73, 83, 97, 100
"Overland Campaign," 77

patriotism, 14, 25–27, 31, 41, 64, 65, 72, 99
Pegram, John, 103, 105, 132n9
Pegram, William Johnson, 61
Pennsylvania Infantry Regiment: 151st, 56
Petersburg: siege of, 85–86, 91–92, 94–97, 99–103, 107–12
Peyton, Aquilla J., 21, 38
Peyton, Charles, 83–84
Peyton, George Quintas, 80, 82, 87–88, 94
Pickett, George Edward, 64
Pitts, Drayton S., 96, 100, 107, 132n16
Pittsylvania County, 26, 75
Pleasonton, Alfred, 84
pneumonia, 20
Pocahontas County, W.Va., 122n11
poetry, 18, 25, 26, 42–43, 54
Point Lookout Prison, Md., 20
Pope, John, 50
Port Republic, 46
Portsmouth, 9, 53, 73, 76, 92, 118
Prince George County, 23, 24, 47, 105
prisoners of war, 20, 33, 68, 85–86, 105–6
Puckett, Henry Douglas, 59
Pulaski County, 106

Randolph, Buckner McGill, 104
Randolph, Robert, 106
Randolph, Thomas Hugh Burwell, 105–6
Raphine, 111
Rapidan Station, 66, 68
Rappahannock Station, 98
rations. *See* food
Reed, James Clayton, 101
religious faith, 21–22, 32, 44, 49, 64, 66, 68, 75
Republican Party, 23, 31, 54
Rhode Island Infantry Regiment: 2nd, 19
Richmond: activity at, 42, 84, 105, 112, 119, 123n16; described, 32–33, 41, 67–68, 75, 117
Robertson, Elizabeth Lee, 11
Rockbridge County, 36, 66, 99, 102, 108
romance, 16, 29, 33, 40, 59, 69, 76, 100, 106
rumors, 26, 33–34, 123–24n33
Runkle, Milton Denton Lewis, 20, 33, 40, 91
Rupert, Jessie, 79

Savage, George Golden, 107
Scates, James Madison, 41
Scott, Winfield, 26
Scottsville, 107, 132n15
Seiders, Alexander H., 20, 56
Seven Pines, 45, 104, 125n22
Shenandoah County, 73, 129n6
Shenandoah Valley: 1862 campaign in, 43–44, 46; 1864 campaign in, 90, 93–95
Sheridan, Philip Henry, 84, 93–94,

107, 110
Sherman, William Tecumseh, 107, 108, 116
Shirley Plantation, 84
shoes, 39, 51, 52, 102, 126n42
sickness, 19–20, 29, 33, 34, 36, 39, 53, 54, 83, 85, 124n38. *See also specific illnesses such as* diarrhea *and* typhoid fever
Silver Spring, Md., 88
smallpox, 20, 59
Snyder, Betty Gray Fitzhugh, 15, 25, 47, 49, 52–53, 57, 61, 68, 73
South Carolina Unit: Holcombe Legion, 96, 100
Southampton County, 27
Spotsylvania, 77, 82, 120, 129n7
Springfield, 31
Staunton, 24, 94
Stevens, George Thomas, 78
Stiles, Robert, 92
Stirewalt, Jacob L., 79
Stone, John H., 16, 21, 53
Stonewall Brigade, 114
Stuart, Alexander Hugh Holmes, 24
Stuart, James Ewell Brown, 28, 62
Suffolk, 40
surgeons, 20, 24, 32, 40, 45, 53, 114, 121n10
Sussex County, 96

Thomas, Charles W., 19–20, 34, 85, 86, 94
Thomas, Mary Rebecca, 29
Todd's Tavern, 82
Totopotomoy Creek, 120
Trowbridge, John Townsend, 117
typhoid fever, 20, 36, 40

uniforms, 123n16

Van Lear, Ausbert George Lewis, 61

vandalism. *See* atrocities
Vanfleet, Abraham, 31–32
Verdiersville, 18
Vicksburg, Miss., 65
Virginia: appearance, 49, 117; importance of, 8–9, 22–23, 117–18; prewar years, 14; secession convention of, 24–25. *See also* atrocities.
Virginia Artillery Units: 12th Light, 86; 19th Heavy, 107; Bedford Artillery, 101; Charlottesville Artillery, 131n59; Chew's Battery, 62, 78, 83, 114; Fluvanna Artillery, 75; Middlesex Artillery, 66, 68; Page's Battery, 63; Richmond Howitzers, 99, 112, 114; Salem Flying Artillery, 113–14; Staunton Hill Battery, 41, 52
Virginia Beach, 8
Virginia Cavalry Regiments: 1st, 16, 29, 30, 31, 36; 2nd, 16, 18, 48, 53; 3rd, 22, 97; 6th, 27, 83, 97; 8th, 113; 11th, 18; 12th, 28; 14th, 89, 122n10; 23rd, 73
Virginia Infantry Regiments: 1st, 29, 46, 63–64, 80–81, 108, 113, 123n16; 3rd, 26, 73, 97; 4th, 46, 130n40; 5th, 22, 96, 101, 102, 108, 111; 6th, 14; 8th, 9, 36, 37, 45; 13th, 33, 80, 82–84, 87, 93–94; 18th, 20; 21st, 58, 114; 27th, 66; 28th, 48; 29th, 40; 30th, 21, 55; 33rd, 34, 73; 34th, 20, 33, 40, 91; 36th, 106; 37th, 88, 119; 40th, 41, 58, 64; 42nd, 43, 49, 59, 111; 45th, 90, 93, 128n1; 49th, 104; 51st, 16, 21, 54, 59, 66, 80, 90, 99, 129n17; 52nd, 37, 39, 90, 103, 109; 55th, 38, 45, 51, 67, 131; 56th, 19, 20, 34, 38, 85, 94; 57th, 35, 86, 92; 59th, 96, 97; 61st, 15, 60
Virginia Military Institute, 27, 29, 79, 87, 89

Walker, John Floyd, 35
Walter, Franklin Gardner, 77–78
Walthall, Howard Malcolm, 29, 30–31, 64, 79–80, 81, 103, 108, 110, 113, 123n16
Walthall, Robert Ryland, 80, 81
Warrenton, 19, 42, 47, 52, 57, 61, 73
Warwick, James Wood, Jr., 18
Washington, D.C., 26, 33, 47, 67; raid on, 87–88, 90, 130n43
Washington College, 111, 130
Washington County, 128
water, 34, 80, 83, 108
Watkins, Frederick William, 31, 32, 47, 55
Waynesboro, 102
weather, 34, 39, 42, 49, 50, 58, 84, 86, 102, 124n1
Wells, Matthew B., 58
West, William M., 118
Westmoreland County, 65, 96–97
Wharton, Gabriel Colvin, 90
Whetzel, Morris, 73
White, James Jones, 87, 130n40
White Oak Road, 132n16
Whitman, Walt, 10–11
whooping cough, 21
Wilderness, 22, 61, 77
Williamsburg, 43, 125n15
Willis, David R., 46
Winchester, 33, 43, 44, 85, 91, 93, 94, 128n3
Wythe County, 16, 42, 66, 90, 95

Zeiler, Ferdinand, 79